christian zen

CHRISTIAN ZEN

William Johnston

1817

HARPER & ROW, PUBLISHERS, San Francisco
Cambridge, Hagerstown, Philadelphia, New York
London, Mexico City, São Paulo, Sydney

Second, revised edition

Designed by

Library of Congress Cataloging in Publication Data

Johnston, William, 1925–
    Christian Zen.

    1. Meditation.   2. Contemplation.   3.Christianity
and other religions—Zen Buddhism.   4. Zen Buddhism—
Relations—Christianity.   I. Title.
BV4813.J63   1981   248.3'4   80–8430
ISBN 0–06–064198–3

---

83 84 10 9 8 7 6 5 4 3

For
  George
  Isidore
  John
  Rich
  and even
  for Pier Paolo

CONTENTS

Some Japanese Words Used in the Text

bonyari	idle
dokusan	private interview
gedo Zen	unorthodox Zen
hakama	divided skirt, traditionally worn by Japanese men
koan	paradoxical problem
kyosaku	stick
makyo	illusion
mu	nothing
muga	non-self
nembutsu	repeating the name of the Buddha
oshosan	priest in charge of a temple
roshi	Zen Master
sake	Japanese rice wine
satori	enlightenment
seiza	traditional Japanese sitting posture
sesshin	retreat (usually seven days)
shikan taza	just sitting
tatami	matting used in Japanese room
teisho	sermon
zazen	sitting in zen meditation

PREFACE TO THE SECOND EDITION

Almost ten years have elapsed since this book was first written, and I know that I could not write the same book today. When questioned about one of his early works, Thomas Merton remarked: " The man who wrote that book is dead." Indeed, Merton the writer died and rose many times, as does every author who lives and grows and develops. That is why I can borrow his words and say that the man who wrote *Christian Zen* is dead.

Yet even if the man who wrote this book is dead, it is also true that he is alive. And as I glance through these pages I realize, sometimes with a jolt, that most of my ideas remain basically unchanged. Some were discarded, only to be taken up again. Others hopefully have deepened and developed. But all in all I can still stand by what I wrote in the fall of 1970.

At that time the great meditation movement which subsequently spread to the whole western world was in its early phase. Transcendental meditation and yoga and Zen were already in vogue. Christians were asking if it was possible for them to avail of the riches of oriental spirituality while remaining committed to Christ and to the Gospel. And to this I wanted to answer that Christians might not only avail of the riches of oriental meditation but that they should become leaders in a movement of which Christ would be the center— a meditation movement which would humbly learn from Zen and the East while being totally penetrated by the Gospel.

I still think this. And in this second edition of *Christian Zen* I have written a fairly long postscript which contains practical instruction on the art of Christian meditation in an oriental setting. Furthermore towards the end of this postscript I describe how my own relationship with Zen developed after publication of this book.

Only one thing would I change if I were to rewrite this book; and this concerns not Zen but Ireland. Here and there I made slightly flippant remarks about the sectarian trouble in the part of the world where I was born. Now I ask my reader to recall that when this book was written the violence had not escalated to the cruel and tragic proportions which we later saw—and which caused untold suffering to many. When I wrote it was possible to laugh at the whole thing. It is no longer a joke.

No more need be said. Here only let me express my belief that authentic Christian meditation is a key factor in healing the wounds of a divided society. For meditation is inextricably bound up with reconciliation and forgiveness and the prayer of Jesus that we may all be one.

Sophia University
Tokyo, 1979

CHAPTER 1

BEGINNING

Some years ago, Arnold Toynbee declared that when the historian of a thousand years from now comes to write the history of our time, he will be preoccupied not with the Vietnam war, not with the struggle between capitalism and communism, not with racial strife, but with what happened when for the first time Christianity and Buddhism began to penetrate one another deeply. This remark is profoundly interesting and, I believe, profoundly true. Christianity and Buddhism are penetrating one another, talking to one another, learning from one another. Even the stubborn old Catholic Church, in a flush of postconciliar humility, feels that she has something to gain by sitting at the feet of the Zen *roshi* and imbibing the age-old wisdom of the East. Surely this is progress.

I have called this little book *Christian Zen*, but the contents are less ambitious than the pretentious title might suggest. Rather than treating of the confluence of two vast traditions of East and West, I simply try to say something about how Zen and Christianity have met in me, setting down some practical conclusions that this meeting has evoked. In the twenty years that I have spent in Japan—so meaningful and rich that this land is almost my land—I have had some contact with Zen, whether by sitting in Zen meditation or through dialogue with my Buddhist friends. All this has been tremendously enriching; it has deepened and broadened my Christian faith more than I can say. Indeed, I

2 *Christian Zen*

sometimes reflect (not without dismay) that had I remained in my native Ireland instead of coming to the East, I might now be an intolerant and narrow-minded Papist hurling bricks and bottles at my Protestant adversaries in the cobbled streets of Belfast. Contact with Zen, on the other hand, has opened up new vistas, teaching me that there are possibilities in Christianity I never dreamed of. It is about this I want to write. So this is a personal book about what I have gained and about the problems that face the person who wants to practice Zen without rejecting his Christian faith—or more correctly, to practice Zen as a way of deepening and broadening his Christian faith. For inevitably the Christian who does Zen hits up against problems. He is faced with a method of meditation that at first sight looks atheistic or pantheistic or whatever you want to call it.

People have frequently asked me why I got interested in Zen at all, and as so often happens, this question is far from easy to answer. Who knows why he gets interested in anything? Yet I suppose some reasons can be given, even though I cannot vouch for the fact that they are the real ones.

For one thing, the contemplative ideal in Buddhism has always fascinated me. I never tire of gazing at the statues of Buddhas and Bodhisattvas rapt in deep silence, in nothingness, in unknowing. They remind me of the exquisite words in which John of the Cross describes contemplative experience:

> Silent music, sounding solitude,
> The supper that recreates and enkindles love.

And then there is the gentle smile of compassion that so often plays around the lips of the Bodhisattva. All this is beautiful. And it reflects the great Buddhist intuition that the highest wisdom is found not in Cartesian clear and distinct ideas but in the tranquil silence that transcends all thoughts, all images, all ideas, all reasoning, in the total extinction of craving and desire. This is what shines through the exquisite silence of the Buddha, a silence that echoes through every corner of Asia.

As I have said, all this attracted me. Consequently, when one of my students offered to bring me to Engakuji, the big Zen temple at Kamakura, I jumped at the opportunity of going there to sit in meditation. At that time it seemed somewhat strange to Christians—and also to non-Christians—that a Catholic priest should meditate in a Zen temple. It seemed like mixing things up; Japanese Christians themselves were vaguely pleased but vaguely puzzled. On the other hand, these were the years leading up to Vatican II, years in which it was becoming increasingly clear that Christians must recognize and promote the true values in religions other than their own. Besides, it was also becoming obvious, alas, that Christianity had failed in Asia mainly because of its intransigent refusal to learn from the local culture and religion. There could be no hope for an Asian Christianity which ignored things like Zen or looked on them with hostility. Other priests had been meditating in Zen temples. Catholicism was on the move.

So I went to Engakuji for several hours on Sunday afternoons, and the young *oshosan* who took care of one of the little temples in the vast complex kindly taught me how to sit.

I was greatly taken by him. A stocky, broad-shouldered ascetic from Okinawa, he was barefoot and dressed in the traditional Japanese *hakama*. Up and down the meditation hall he crept silently, ready to strike or to scold with the utmost severity. But when the meditation was over and we drank green tea together, he radiated all the gentleness and compassion of the great Bodhisattvas.

One day he called me aside. "Thank you so much for coming," he said. "Now I would like to see a Christian monastery."

I was somewhat taken aback. I felt that there was not in Tokyo a

Christian monastery to which I could introduce him with reasonable hope that he would be edified. Plenty of Christian contemplatives there were (more indeed among the Japanese than elsewhere), but our monasteries were so Western, so much like offices—and he would probably have to wear shoes. The incident made me realize how great is the need for contemplative renewal within Christianity and how much can be learnt from Buddhism.

But to return to the meditation. Soon I found myself together with a small group of people sitting in the half-lotus position and gazing at the wall in silence. This kind of meditation was not, however, entirely new to me. John of the Cross had been my guru for many years, and at this time I was reading *The Cloud of Unknowing* (about which I subsequently wrote a somewhat academic book), which teaches a species of silent, imageless meditation not unlike Zen. At the beginning of one of his minor treatises, for example, the anonymous author of *The Cloud* confronts his disciples with the stern words: "When thou comest by thyself . . . forsake as well good thoughts as evil thoughts." The author's idea is that all discursive thinking should be abandoned in order that an interior dynamism (which he beautifully calls "the blind stirring of love") may arise in the depth of one's being. His doctrine resembles that of John of the Cross in advocating abandonment of thinking in order to make way for what the Spanish mystic calls "the living flame of love."

I might add here that imageless prayer is not uncommon among Christians devoted to meditation, but there is not much talk about it. One time, while conducting a retreat for sisters in the south of Japan, I suggested that we spend some hours in silent, Zenlike meditation, gazing at the wall. After this experiment, quite a few of the sisters remarked, "But I always meditate that way anyhow."

And the same was true for me when I first went to Kamakura.

As far as interior disposition was concerned I changed nothing; but I found that I was enormously helped and, so to speak, deepened simply by the half-lotus posture which I then took on for the first time. After an unbearably painful beginning (for some strange reason I always got a headache), I began to realize that this is indeed the ideal posture for contemplative prayer—for putting into practice the advice of the good author of *The Cloud* to "forsake as well good thoughts as evil thoughts." The fact is that this lotus position somehow impedes discursive reasoning and thinking; it somehow checks the stream of consciousness that flows across the surface of the mind; it detaches one from the very process of thinking. Probably it is the worst position for philosophizing but the best for going down, down to the center of one's being in imageless and silent contemplation. This position had the further simple advantage of keeping me quiet, since a certain nervous restlessness had made me want to pace up and down my room in time of so-called meditation. Now I found myself rooted to the earth in silent unification.

The Kamakura experience somehow helped my daily meditation, which I continued to make in the half-lotus position (I could never manage the full lotus—alas for Western legs) in some kind of Zen style. I say this because some people would probably deny that what I did was Zen, and whether or not it could be called Zen I did not know. As I have already said, it was a continuation, but at the same time a remarkable deepening, of what I had been doing before I ever heard of Zen.

After some time I attended my first Zen *sesshin* (that is to say, a retreat) at a small temple on the Japan Sea. This was an unforgettable experience, though the whole thing was very severe and grueling. Perhaps I was not yet ready for it. We arose at 3 A.M., sat in *zazen* for ten periods of forty minutes each, and retired at 9 P.M. Even our meals were taken in the lotus posture

in the meditation hall. During the time allotted to the reciting
of the sutras, a Jesuit colleague and I were kindly permitted to
celebrate Mass, which we did in the small *tatami* room that had
been given to us. Each morning the *roshi* gave an instruction,
called *teisho*, in which he expounded some of the principles of
Buddhist philosophy in addition to giving hints for the practice
of Zen. In one of these instructions he remarked that Zen was
found everywhere and in all true religions—in Hinduism, in
Islam, in Christianity, and so on. Such Zen he called *"gedo* Zen."
"Ge" means outside, and *"do"* means the way; so *"gedo* Zen"
is unorthodox or heretical Zen. The real Zen, he went on to say,
was not Hinayana nor even Mahayana—it was just Zen divorced
from all categories and affiliations. I was interested to hear that
he did concede that there was Zen in every religion, and this
made me think that what I was doing might be called Zen after all.

In the course of another *teisho* he spoke about *dokusan* or
spiritual direction. This, he explained, was usually a brief affair
and dealt only with the actual practice of Zen. "I don't want to
hear about your financial problems," he said, "nor about your
family problems. And if you talk about these things I'll stop you.
All I want to know is what you are doing during your *zazen*."
To me this simple remark was quite striking, and I felt it could
give Christian directors food for thought. As a seminarian study-
ing for the priesthood, I had frequently gone to spiritual directors and found their attitude the contrary of that of the *roshi*. They
asked about practical problems of adjustment to life, and by and
large they were good counselors; but they shied away from the
central problem of "What are you doing at the time of meditation?" Perhaps this stemmed from a natural reluctance to talk
about something sacred. Yet it is true that we can all learn much
from the Zen *roshi*, who know about the working of the human

mind in an intimate way. That is why they can lead persons to *satori*.

Anyhow, I squatted in the queue, and when my time came I struck the gong and went in for *dokusan*. The *roshi* was seated on a slightly raised platform, and down below, some distance away, was the cushion on which I was to squat. I wondered why he was so far away; later I put this question to a Japanese who knew the temple pretty well. Almost furtively he said, "I'll tell you the reason. The *roshi* drinks sake, and he doesn't want you to smell his breath." Seeing my surprise he went on hastily, "I don't mean that he drinks too much. He doesn't. But he drinks some, and he doesn't like people to know."

I reflected that, after all, Zen *roshi* were human beings, good men like the Irish Catholic pastors. As for my conversation with the *roshi* it was, as far as I recall, more or less as follows.

"How are you getting on?"

"My legs are aching so much that I can scarcely bear it any longer."

"Stretch them out! Stretch them out! I'll tell the young man in the meditation hall not to bother you. If the thing is too painful, you'll simply give it up. And I don't want you to give it up, I want you to continue. So don't overdo it. But tell me, what about your Zen? What are you doing?"

"I'm doing what you, I suppose, would call '*gedo* Zen.' "

"Very good! Very good! Many Christians do that. But what precisely do you mean by '*gedo* Zen'?"

"I mean that I am sitting silently in the presence of God without words or thoughts or images or ideas."

"Your God is everywhere?"

"Yes"

"And you are wrapped around in God?"

"Yes"

"And you experience this?"

"Yes"

"Very good! Very good! Continue this way. Just keep on. And eventually you will find that God will disappear and only Johnston San will remain."

This remark shocked me. It sounded like a denial of all that I considered sacred, of all that lay at the very center of my so-called Zen. One should not, I suppose, contradict the *roshi*, but nevertheless I did so. Recalling the teaching of *The Cloud* that there are mystical moments when self totally disappears and only God remains, I said with a smile, "God will not disappear. But Johnston might well disappear and only God be left."

"Yes, yes," he answered smilingly. "It's the same thing. That is what I mean."

Yet, as I have said, his seemingly radical denial of God was a shock to me. But afterward, reflecting on the whole matter and discussing it with my friends, I came to the conclusion that his words did not necessarily deny the existence of God at all. Underlying them is a denial of dualism and an approach to God which is different from that of the traditional West. Now I maintain that this way of speaking throws light on the very notion of God, helping Western Christians to purify and clarify their ideas. But this realization only came later, and the remark of the *roshi* shook me.

All this happened some years ago. Today Zen has entered Christianity with more confidence. Outside Tokyo there is now a simply built Christian Zen meditation hall in which are conducted monthly *sesshin*. In the center of Tokyo (yes—noisy, dirty, smoggy, grimy Tokyo) is a quiet place where Christians and others come to sit in silence. In sitting together with these young Japanese people, it has never been my intention to guide and instruct them in Zen; all I have wanted is to be with them and to learn. I have told Japanese Christians—and I believe it is true—that they have an important role to play in the development of Christianity. Their vocation is to renew meditation within the Church and interpret it to the West. At the same time they must humbly and gratefully acknowledge their debt to Buddhism, as I myself must express my gratitude for the unfailing kindness and courtesy with which my friends and I have always been treated by Zen *roshi*.

Renewal of meditation in Christianity! There has, after all, been renewal in almost every other field. The organ has been replaced by the guitar; ties have replaced Roman collars; nuns' skirts have moved from maxi to mini and back to midi; scriptural and theological progress has been breath-taking. But surely all this progress will be so much junk (if I may be pardoned the word) if religion is not renewed at its very heart, that is to say, at the mystical level. That such renewal is badly overdue is proved by the fact that many people, discontented with old forms of prayer, discontented with the old devotions that once served so well, are looking for something that will satisfy the aspirations of the modern heart.

And is it not just possible that the vocation of the East lies here?

CHAPTER 2

DIALOGUE

One of the beautiful things of our age—which, alas, has all kinds of ugly things also—is that we have learned to talk to one another. Slowly we are mastering the art of dialogue. And the religions of the world, after centuries of rivalry and quarreling, are learning to wipe the blood off their hands, beat their swords into plowshares, and exchange the kiss of peace. Truly an interesting and exciting age.

Since I myself hail from such a bigoted and intolerant corner of the earth, I have always felt that dialogue with other religions is something of a sacred duty. Somehow I ought to make amends. That is why I have been so glad to attend meetings between Christians and Zen Buddhists that have taken place in various parts of Japan. Most of these meetings have been more or less unofficial (that is to say, the people present were not officially appointed by central religious authorities) and have been conducted in a spirit of the utmost cordiality and friendship. We meet on terms of equality—no attempt, of course, is made at proselytizing—in the belief that none of us possess the totality of the truth. To us Catholic Christians the Vatican Council brought the refreshing news that we are still seekers, members of a pilgrim Church, and so we can join hands with other searchers, whether they be Buddhist, Hindu, Muslim, or anything else, in our common quest for truth. Needless to say, we have Christ, who I believe spoke of God as no man ever spoke; but I do not think we can claim to understand the revelation of Christ in all its fullness. Perhaps we are still at the beginning. Moreover I also believe that in sundry times and in diverse ways God spoke to our fathers through the prophets, and these include prophets whose voices echo beautifully in the *Gita*, the *Lotus Sutra*, and the *Tao Teh Ching*.

I am aware that it sounds awfully patronizing to give Christianity the plum of Divine Sonship and throw a few crumbs of prophethood to Buddhists and Hindus, but I have found that Buddhists, at least those I have met and know, do not take this amiss. They want to know what we think without camouflage or dilution, and in the same way we want to know what they think. None of the Christians are particularly disturbed to hear that they possess the Buddha nature. The fact is, however, that we are only now advancing from the backwoods of intolerance and have not yet found a formula that will keep everyone happy. Perhaps we never will.

The dialogue with Zen owes much to the initiative and enterprise of the Quakers, to whom we are all eternally grateful. No doubt the great similarity between Quaker meditation and Zen (though there are great differences too) was instrumental in prompting their ecumenical interest. The first meeting was held in Oiso, near Tokyo, and the participants talked frankly about their personal religious experience, searching for a link that might bind them together. Conducted in a spirit of great charity, it revealed that the interior life of Buddhists and Christians has much in common; they can be united at the deepest part of their being, at the level of psychic life which Eliot calls the still point of the turning world. But the participants were unable to enunciate any theological or philosophical statement all could agree upon.

When the time came round for the next meeting, this time to be held in Kyoto, it seemed to me that we should leave the subjective realm of religious experience and get down to something objective. Perhaps the whole discussion could center around the problem of ultimate reality—we Christians could explain what we meant by "God," pointing out that we did not believe in an anthropomorphic being "out there" but in the supreme source of existence in whom we live, move, and are. The Buddhists, on the other hand, could explain what they mean by nothingness, emptiness, the void, and so on. In this way a lot of misunderstanding might vanish like smoke; we might discover that we had something in common after all, and what a break-through this would be in religious thinking! Now I realize that I was naïve. Or a victim of my Hellenistic education.

Anyhow, with this in mind I spoke to a Buddhist friend who was to be a participant. He listened kindly, and his answer, typically Buddhist and deeply interesting, was more or less as follows. "Do you really think that you can talk about nothingness, emptiness, or the void? Do you really think you can talk about God? Of course you can't. You are part of the void; you are part of nothingness; you are part of God. All is one."

And here I found clearly and directly expressed something that runs all through Zen, whether it be in the thinking of the simplest Master or the most sophisticated scholar: that is to say, there is no duality, no "I and Thou" (alas for Martin Buber), no "God and myself." All is one. This is the so-called monism that underlies all Mahayana Buddhism. Let me illustrate it further with a story about the great Dr. Suzuki.

One time the old philosopher gave a talk on Zen to Western people in Tokyo. He spoke of the silence, the emptiness, the nothingness, and all the rest, together with the deep wisdom that comes from *satori*. When he had finished, one of his audience rose to his feet and, not without a touch of irritation, exclaimed,

"But Dr. Suzuki, what about society? What about other people? What about the other?"

Whereupon Suzuki paused for a moment, looked up with a smile, and remarked, "But there is no other!"

There is no other, and there is no self. This is the answer he had to give, and this basically was the answer of my Buddhist friend. What they meant by it (for it is by no means as simple or as terrible as it sounds) I would like to discuss later; for the present, let us return to the dialogue.

We met in Kyoto, where we spent a wonderful week, fifteen of us. The atmosphere was permeated with good will and deep religious faith. Not only did we talk together, we also sat together in a wordless dialogue of silent communication. The meeting was highlighted by a talk from an eminent *roshi* who described with great enthusiasm the experience of enlightenment that had made him wild with ecstatic joy. His head seemed to be shattered and for several days he did not know where he was or what he was doing. *Satori* could never be described or explained, he said, but there was undoubtedly enlightenment in the words of Jesus:

Before Abraham was, I am.

This, he said, was perfect enlightenment—no object, no duality, just "I am."

Here I might digress to say that I have been impressed and moved by the respect and reverence with which Buddhists have always spoken of Christ in my presence. However dim a view they may take of us, and I suppose they have reason on occasion, they have not concealed their admiration for the founder of Christianity. In this case his words gave me food for thought. I had heard it said before that "I am" is an expression of perfect *satori*. It should be noted, however, that when the words "I am" rise up in the depth of the enlightened being, this "I" is not the empirical ego; it is not the little self that is compounded of desires and does not really exist in Zen. This "I" is the very ground of being, the heart of the universe, the true self which rises in the depths and overwhelms everything. It is the voice of the "big self" which drowns all consciousness of the "little self" because it is all that is. I saw then clearly that when Jesus said "I am," the "I" that spoke was not the "I" of a man, but that of the eternal Word that was in the beginning and through whom all things were made. Jesus, I believe, was so filled with God that he no longer had a human personality—within him was only the personality of the eternal Son. That is why the "I" that cried out within him was the same as that which spoke to Moses saying, "I am who I am."

Be that as it may, our talk has gone on over cups of coffee and green tea, while at other times it has been more formal, with tape recorders and press correspondents. Perhaps the reader will ask where it is all going and what we are getting out of it. Yet this is, perhaps, a question no one can answer. In some ways dialogue is a dangerous and tricky business. At one meeting a Buddhist professor humorously made the remark that we all feel the cultural and religious danger. After all, if you leave yourself open, if you recognize the other's position, if you treat with others on terms of equality—then God alone knows what might happen. But the risk is worth taking, and progress will be made. As for myself, my principal preoccupation at present is with learning from Buddhism. I can't help feeling that Western Christianity (like Western everything else) is badly in need of a blood transfusion. Somehow or other we have become effete—is this the old theory about the decline of the West?—and we need new perspectives. Just as a whole new era opened up for Christianity when Thomas introduced Aristotle in the thirteenth century, so a new era, an even bigger one, could be opened up by the assimilation of some Buddhist ideas and attitudes. And the time is particularly ripe for this now that we see Christianity as an open-ended religion, a religion on the march, a religion that has taken things from Hellenism and communism and will only reach something like completion when it sees the truth through the eyes of all cultures. Indeed, it is precisely because of its claim to universality that Christianity needs the insights of other religions. And here I might add that many Buddhists I have met are also on the march, happy and willing to learn from Christianity.

But now about the blood transfusion. What can Christians learn from Zen? Or in a book like this it might be better to ask what I have learned, or am in the process of learning, from Zen. And first of all it seems to me that Zen can teach us a methodology in prayer. Let me explain what I mean.

Every religion that is worth its salt has taught people how to pray. Some religions are poor in theology and organization; but if they have prayer or meditation we can respect them and recognize that they are trying to do their job. In Buddhism and Hinduism there have always been people—gurus and *roshi*—who have so mastered the art of meditation that they can lead their disciples through the tortuous paths of the mind to a high level of concentration. Now Christianity, too, has a similar tradition (how could it otherwise have survived?), as also has Judaism. Recall how the disciples said to Jesus, "Teach us to pray, as John taught his disciples to pray." They expected Jesus to be a Master of prayer, as were John and the other rabbis who moved around the countryside. The fathers of the Church, too, taught prayer; and later on we find men like Ignatius of Loyola wandering around Paris simply instructing people in the ways of meditation. Ignatius had a method—it is outlined in his *Spiritual Exercises*—and he aimed at bringing people to something like *satori*. His method continues and flourishes even today.

Yet the method of Ignatius was grossly misunderstood, and became tied up with rationalism, with reasoning and thinking and a so-called "discursive prayer" that appeals little to modern man, who wants mysticism. Modern people, like Hamlet, have had too many words, words, words. Perhaps it is that they are wrung out and exhausted by television, radio, advertising, and all the stuff that McLuhan calls the extension of man's nervous system throughout our planet. What they want is deep interior silence. And this can be found through Zen, as it could be found through Ignatius' method if it were properly understood. Zen has simple techniques, however, for introducing people to inner peace and even to the so-called Christian "infused contemplation." The Japanese, as is well known in the world of economics, are an eminently practical people, and they have perfected the Zen method that came to birth in China: the sitting, the breathing, the control of the mind.

But the key thing in Zen is not just sitting in the lotus posture. The key (or so it seems to me) is detachment, the art of which is highly developed in Zen. It should be remembered that all forms of Buddhism are built on detachment and that the roots of Zen are here.

"What then is the Holy Truth of the Origination of Ill? It is that craving which leads to rebirth, accompanied by delight and greed, seeking its delight now here, now there, i.e., craving for sensuous experience, craving to perpetuate oneself, craving for extinction.

"What then is the Holy Truth of the Stopping of Ill? It is the complete stopping of that craving, the withdrawal from it, the renouncing of it, throwing it back, liberation from it, nonattachment to it."

True to these principles, Zen inculcates a renunciation or asceticism that is truly extraordinary. One must be detached from everything, even from oneself. Nor does Zen detachment simply mean doing without alcohol and tobacco (this is the usual Christian understanding of the word); it goes much deeper to include detachment from the very process of thinking, from the images and ideas and conceptualization that are so dear to Western man. And through this detachment one is introduced to a deep and beautiful realm of psychic life. One goes down, down to the depths of one's being—or, if you want a Zen physiological explanation, to the pit of one's stomach. As the process continues, one becomes detached even in those subliminal regions in which are found infantile fixations, unconscious drives, and all the rest. When detachment sets in here, Zen has something in common with psychoanalysis and can even be therapeutic for those who are able and willing to take the medicine. But I have written about this in my little book *The Still Point* and need not repeat it here. All I want to say is that so far as detachment is concerned it resembles greatly the Christian contemplative path of John of the Cross. So striking indeed is the similarity that some scholars hold that John of the Cross received Buddhist influence through Neoplatonism. But this is by no means certain.

Anyhow, detachment is only one side of the coin. One becomes detached in order that something else may shine forth. In the Buddhist this is his Buddha nature. For, contrary to what is often said, true Zen is based on a very great faith—faith in the presence of the Buddha nature in the deepest recesses of the personality; faith that, as the Four Noble Truths point out, there is a way out of the morass of suffering and that man can be transformed through enlightenment. I believe this point is worth stressing for one frequently hears that there are in Zen no faith, no presuppositions, "no dependence on words and letters." In one sense this is all true. It is true that no conceptualized system can be present in the mind in time of *zazen*; it is also true that one cannot point to any one sutra and say, "Here is the essence of Zen." But in spite of this the fact remains that the whole thing is penetrated with the spirit of Buddhism, the spirit of the patriarchs, the spirit of the sutras. If one speaks to Zen people one finds this immediately; if one listens to the talks in the temples it is quite clear. There is a great faith here.

In Christian Zen this faith may take the form of a conviction that God is present in the depth of my being or, put in other words, that I am made in the image of God. Or it may express itself in the Pauline words, "I live, now not I; but Christ lives in me." The deepest and truest thing within me is not myself but God. As Christian Zen develops, self disappears (here is the Christian *muga* or nonself situation), and God lives and acts within me; my activity is no longer my own but the activity of God who is all in all. In the last analysis there is nothing except God. Paul says that there is nothing except Christ. "There is no such thing as Jew and Greek, slave and freeman, male and female; for you are all one in Christ." This is how Christian Zen will develop. The point I have tried to make here, for I consider it important, is that some kind of faith is necessary in a practice like Zen, and that one is not floating in the air as much as some people have said. This is true of all forms of deep meditation, and it is probably for this reason that a man like Aldous Huxley, who had great interest in meditation but no particular belief in anything, just didn't get anywhere. You can't go on detaching yourself indefinitely in the hope that something may or may not turn up inside. One may of course begin meditation without much faith, and many of the people who come to our place in Tokyo do just that, but the time comes when faith is necessary, and without it no one goes through to the end.

In short, it seems to me that Christians can profit greatly from Zen methodology to deepen their Christian faith, and here in Japan an increasing number of Christians, both Japanese and Western, are discovering this. A growing number of Catholic Japanese nuns, for example, are quietly practising Zen, and I believe it has a future within the Church. Surely it would be a good idea to take up this methodology and start once again teaching people how to pray. For the sad fact is that, while Catholic monks and nuns are teaching all kinds of things from botany to business English, not many are teaching people how to pray.

There is, of course, more to the methodology than the couple of points I have mentioned; but I think it better to leave the discussion of the *roshi* and the *koan* to a later chapter. What I want to say here is that impoverished Western man is greatly in need of something like this, because the contemplative life is fantastically underdeveloped in the developed and affluent nations. Western civilization has become horribly one-sided and unbalanced, so much so that serious people cannot see the distinction between a computer and a man. When this happens, and when the contemplative dimension existing in every man becomes starved, then people go berserk and do crazy things. And this is what is happening. Moreover it is ghastly to think that it is happening even among some monks and nuns. Here are people whose lives are geared to *satori*, yet they feel that all is meaningless unless they are moving around the place making noise in the name of Christian charity.

If young people look to Hinduism and Buddhism for the contemplative education that they instinctively long for, may this not be because modern Christianity has projected the image of a churchgoing religion rather than a mystical one? May it not have too much bingo and too little mysticism? Too much theological chatter and not enough subliminal silence? Words, words, words! Perhaps this is why we need the blood transfusion from the East.

There are other important lessons to be learned from Zen, which I shall take up in the next chapter.

CHAPTER 3

MONISM AND DUALISM

From what has been said it will be clear that if Christianity and Buddhism cross spiritual swords, the issue at stake is monism versus dualism. This was the point of the old *roshi* who told me that God would disappear and only Johnston would remain. This again was the point of my friend who said that one cannot even talk about God and Nothingness. The *roshi* was referring to this when he spoke of Christ's enlightenment, expressed in the words "I am." And Dr. Suzuki was getting at this when he said, "But there is no other." So it all comes down to a basic problem: Are there many things or is there only one thing?

The monism versus dualism conflict has, of course, been a live issue in the West for many centuries, and Christians have been warned about the dangers of pantheism and nihilism and all the horrible things for which people like Eckhart were clobbered in the fourteenth century. But now that the pure and fresh breeze of dialogue and tolerance blows through the world, we can begin to ask other questions. We can ask: What is good in this "monism"? What can we learn from it? What does it really mean? Is it really the enemy of Christianity? What message does it have for the West?

Let me immediately give my own answer to this question. I believe that the Christian West needs a touch of this so-called monism. Modern people are looking for it, and most of it can be understood in a Christian sense. This, I believe, was one of the insights of the great Thomas Merton. I had the privilege of meeting the famous Trappist in Gethsemani (though our meeting was sadly brief, as he was called away by the bell), and afterward we exchanged letters. A few days before we were to meet again in Japan I was shocked to hear of his sudden death—electrocuted by a fan in Bangkok. I had kept him informed about our poor Zen efforts, and he followed the whole thing with the keenest interest. Because of legal complications I must paraphrase the letter instead of quoting it directly. This I have done, remaining as faithful as possible to what Merton said.

Dear Father Johnston,

Many thanks for your kind letter. I was interested to hear about the *sesshin*. I myself think that the lotus posture is quite unimportant. But perhaps Father Lasalle and yourself want to look like the real thing in the eyes of the Japanese and for this reason it may have some relevance. The problem of *satori* is more delicate.

Though I am far away and have no direct knowledge of what is going on in Japan, I will attempt to give an opinion that might have some value.

Possibly the Zen people have their own idea of what we mean when we say that we believe in God. Perhaps they think that it necessarily implies dualism and the establishment of an I-Thou relationship—something concerned with subject and object. And of course this would make *satori* impossible. I wonder if they know about Eckhart who says that it is possible to be so poor that one does not even have a God. And Eckhart is not here propounding Christian atheism and the death of God. He is simply speaking about an experience that is found clearly in all forms of apophatic mysticism. Also the Zen people may think about Christian mysticism in terms of the bride and the bridegroom. And this takes us pretty far from *satori* too.

But let's look at the thing from another standpoint. Perhaps someone like Father Lasalle who wants as a Christian to get *satori* ends up in a situation which makes *satori* psychologically impossible. Because to get the true *satori* one must have no plans whatever about a Christian getting *satori*—one must be completely detatched from such plans. Perhaps the Zen people have a kind of intuition that Christians practising Zen are in such a psychological position.

I myself believe that a Christian can get *satori* just as easily as a Buddhist. It is simply a case of going beyond all forms, images, concepts, categories and the rest. But it may be that the type of Christianity we now have makes this difficult. Probably the best thing to do is to use Zen for purposes of inner purification and liberation from system and conceptual thinking without bothering about whether or not we get *satori*. At the same time, if Father Lasalle feels that it is his vocation to get there, I am all for him. Please tell me more about all this. Have the German books Dumoulin and Lasalle been translated into English? I'm trying to review them, but my German is not so good.

> With every best wish,
> Yours in Christ
> THOMAS MERTON

Truth to tell, I don't go along with everything that Merton says in the above letter. Probably the cross-legged position is more important than he thinks—though he is right in saying it is not essential. Again, I don't think that any of us Westerners are particularly anxious to be the real thing in the eyes of the Japanese. And I also think we have always known well enough that the person striving for *satori* with attachment never gets there. So far for my gripes. They are no more than small reservations about the thought of the great man. What he states well and with rough clarity is that Zen goes beyond all categories and all duality and that Christianity can do the same. In certain areas of apophatic experience (the Rhineland mystics make it clear) the subject-object relationship disappears. And this is no mere Christian atheism or denial of God but simply another way of experiencing God. All this is worth saying, and I am so grateful to the busy Merton for taking the trouble to sit down at his typewriter and bash out this letter to me. Let me try to elaborate on his ideas while adding my own.

For the past few centuries popular Christianity has spoken of God in a dualistic and even anthropomorphic way. I say popular Christianity because the mystics like Eckhart, the anonymous author of *The Cloud*, John of the Cross, and the rest were never guilty of this oversimplification. But the popular brand of Christianity preached from the pulpit undoubtedly did tend to speak about the God "out there" that has been pilloried by Robinson in *Honest to God*. Perhaps this was partly due to an interpretation of the Bible that was too fundamentalist, a literal interpretation of the God who walked in the garden with Adam, who was angry with his people, and who is called "Father." Be that as it may, popular Christianity had the strong, if unconscious, tendency to put God *in a place*, and this tendency still persists. How many Christians, even those advanced in interior things, want to put God either above the clouds or (if that is unacceptable to modern man) in the depths of the heart or in the core of the being. But in all such cases God is *somewhere*.

Now it is quite certain that an orthodox Zen monk will deny the existence of such a God; he will say that there is nothing resembling this God in his meditation nor is there any dialogue with a transcendent being. He will even go so far as to say that considerations about such a being destroy Zen. This is completely natural, for he is totally committed to a nondualism. He is the unrelenting opponent of all subject-object relationships; he is against all activity of the discriminating intellect. How could he possibly accept the idea that God is *there* and I am *here*?

And there is, of course, much truth in what he says, as Merton points out. Christians must recall the old, old philosophical truth, stressed and restressed by the mystics and elaborated by good Aquinas himself, that God is not in a place. He is not *there* in the sense that I am *here*. It is true; of course, that we may think of him in a place for convenience' sake, just as we may paint pictures of God the Father. But we must always remember the inadequacy of such an approach, recalling the fact that God is nowhere. He simply is. To put God in a place is to limit and restrict one who by definition is unlimited. If you say God is *there*, you imply that he is not *here*. Which is an absurdity. And perhaps many people saw the absurdity of this and rejected God altogether. Hence the death-of-God wave that burst over the Western world.

Turning to the Christian mystics, however, we find a different story. Here are men and women whose meditation (or contemplation) is more akin to that of the Zen Masters in that it embraces an area of experience which is beyond subject and object. I was particularly impressed by this while writing my book on *The Cloud*. The English author, in one of his minor treatises called *The Epistle of Privy Counsel* (which I recommend to anyone interested in Zen), is no less unrelenting than the Masters in his efforts to withdraw his disciple from subject-object relations. God is your being, he says (not "God is in you or in your being," etc.)—though your being is not the being of God. Simply be! Lose the sense of your own being for a sense of the being of God! This English author stands clearly in the great tradition of "theology of negation" that stems from Dionysius, passes to the Rhenish mystics, and reaches a climax with John of the Cross. Merton, too, belongs to the same tradition, and that is why he has such sympathy for Zen.

It might be argued that this doing away with subject-object relations is not in the Bible, which is dualistic to the hilt. This is sometimes maintained even by great theologians like Karl Barth, who are unvarnished enemies of the Dionysian tradition. They look on the whole apophatic stream culminating in John of the

Cross as a monistic contamination of the beautiful spirituality
that flows from the Bible. But in this I do not go along with them
at all. Because apart from the fact that the Bible is not the whole
of Christianity and necessarily restricts itself to Jewish cultural
patterns—apart from this, if one reads the Bible carefully one
can find there the seeds of the theology of negation. They are
there in embryo. Not that this mystical stuff is expressed in terms
of nothingness and emptiness and the void, because the Jews
just didn't talk that way. But they had their own way of saying
that God is unknowable and that he is not in a place and so on.
This they said by forbidding the making of images, with the
assertion that God is not like any of these things—for no man
has ever seen God. Moreover the story is told—and it is a story
that really appeals to me—that when the victorious Pompey
strode into the Holy of Holies curious to see what was there, he
found nothing (how close at last to Buddhism!). For this was
the Jewish way of proclaiming the supreme unknowability of
God. In addition, the seeds of apophatic mysticism are scattered
throughout *Job* and *Deutero-Isaias* (or so it seems to me).

I say all this because it is of great importance for the dialogue
with Zen and for those Christians who would like to practice
Zen while cleaving to God. It means that it is not necessarily
atheism to say that God will disappear and only Johnston will
remain. It means that Christians can practice Zenlike meditation
being intensely aware of God without making him an object of
thought. God is not, strictly speaking, an object. He is the ground
of being. If this is not grasped, Zen will be called atheistic and
its introduction to Christianity will be roundly opposed or regarded with suspicion.

Nor is this to deny the dualistic aspect of reality, which for
the Christian always remains. And here we come to the famous
problem of "the one and the many," which has occupied the

finest minds in the West from Parmenides and Aristotle to Aquinas. There is one thing; yet there are many things. Such a delicate and difficult problem as this I would not venture to tackle here, even if I had the ability to do so. Suffice it to say that the Aristotelian tradition (which, I believe, has still something to say) holds to both limbs—the one and the many. Though I am not a philosopher I have always thought this eminently sensible, since it tallies with experience. Everyday life tells us that there are many things; experience like Zen tells us that there is one thing. Why not stick to both? Must we deny one area of experience?

The point I want to make here, however, is that Christian prayer must find room for both facets of reality. Like Zen it can be silent, imageless, without subject-object relationship, and beyond dialogue. In this kind of meditation all is one, God is all in all, "I" am lost. Such is the prayer of the mystics. But there can also be dialogue between creature and Creator, made by the creature who raises up his hands like Moses to intercede for his people and for the world. Generally the prayer of Christians advanced in meditation is a mixture of both—it has its moments of imageless silence and its moments of dialogue with the Father. Consequently, coming to practice, I would suggest that Christians who do Zen use both methods of meditation. Let them follow their deepest spiritual instincts, since it is here that the Spirit is working. There will be times when they wish to be totally silent in the absence of subject-object relationship and in interior unification. And then they should follow this inclination. Many Christians educated in the I-Thou dualism have a scruple about doing this (this I have discovered from my Christian friends who do Zen), as if the abandonment of dualism meant the abandonment of God. But they should put aside such scruples. Let them enter into the area of apophatic experience that is, in fact, filled with the beauty and immensity and goodness of God. Even though it is God in darkness. On the other hand, if words of dialogue rise up in the heart—if, for example, they want to repeat the famous "Jesus prayer" or cry out to God; if they want to praise and thank God or make the prayer of petition—let them do so. Let us be for freedom. Let us follow the Spirit.

In this whole matter, however, it should be recalled that dialogue in Christian prayer reaches its perfection when it is no longer "my dialogue with God" but "Christ's dialogue with the Father in me." That is to say, the real Christian prayer is not *my* prayer but Christ's prayer. It is the voice of Christ within my soul crying out, "Abba, Father!" How wonderful this is in Paul! In such prayer we have the nonself (the *muga* or the sanskrit *anatta*), since it is no longer I that live, but Christ that lives in me.

At this point I would like to quote a passage from Gregory of Nyssa, who has been called "the father of Christian mysticism" (though I believe that he isn't—for Christ is the father of Christian mysticism), in which he speaks of the passage through Zen-like silence to the culminating cry of "Abba, Father!"

Then I would leave behind the earth altogether and traverse all the middle air; I would reach the beautiful ether, come to the stars and behold all their orderly array. But not even there would I stop short, but, passing beyond them, would become a stranger to all that moves and changes, and apprehend the stable Nature, the immovable Power which exists in its own right, guiding and keeping in being all things, for all depend on the ineffable will of the Divine Wisdom. So first my mind must become detached from everything subject to flux and change and tranquilly rest in motionless repose, so as to be rendered akin to Him who is perfectly unchangeable; and then it may address Him by this most familiar name and say: Father." *

Here the word "Father" is no simple utterance; it is something

---

* St. *Gregory of Nyssa: The Lord's Prayer*, Hilda C. Graef, trans. and annot. (London: Burns and Oates, 1954), p. 37.

that issues from the depth of one's being when, detached from all things, one rests tranquilly in motionless spiritual repose. Such an experience may seem a thousand miles from Zen, but there are still similarities—not only in the silencing of the faculties, the deep repose, the detachment and the integration, but also in the nonself condition in which the word "Father" rises up in the heart. For, reading Gregory and the mystics in depth, one sees that this cry does not issue from the empirical ego (which has been lost). It is the cry of Christ to his Father, the Son offering himself to the Father in Trinitarian love, the Son who is within as in the Pauline "I live, now not I; but Christ lives in me." So Christian prayer ends up in a Trinitarian context. It ends up with the frightening paradox that there is dialogue within a being that is totally one.

But would it be an oversimplification to say that the East has stressed unity and that the West has stressed diversity? And that they need one another? Or better, to say that the mystic East teaches us in a striking way that all is one, while the scientific West has brilliantly grasped the diversity and the many? And that they need one another. Perhaps we should shy away from such wild generalizations. Yet I like to think this way in our dialogue with Zen.

CHAPTER 4

CHRISTIAN ZEN (1)

During the summer of 1970 I lectured on mysticism in San Francisco. People had told me that California is the center of yoga and witchcraft, Zen and sorcery, drugs and nudity, and everything under the sun. They said that there were all kinds of *swamis* and *roshis*, *gurus* and transcendental meditators floating around the place, and that the atmosphere was haunted by the ghost of Aldous Huxley swallowing mescaline and claiming to have had the Beatific Vision. In short, California was the home of mysticism true and false. Whether or not this is true I do not know. All I know is that I fell in love with the wide open spaces of California and with the breath-taking beauty of Big Sur. I left some of my heart in San Francisco.

I tried to invest my classes with a veneer of academic learning (after all, *noblesse oblige*); but feeling that with such a subject theory must be supplemented by practice, I invited the students, and anyone else who wanted to come, to sit in *zazen* for forty minutes each evening. Obviously it was not my intention to turn them into mystics but merely to give them some tiny experience and savoring of the *silentium mysticum* (this, I believe, is possible) and to introduce them to a meditation that would be without thought, without images, without desire, in interior unification and peace. This I tried to do by developing a few simple techniques, and with a short explanation which I shall outline in a moment. I wanted to have the minimum of theory so that they could just sit.

To my surprise fifty or sixty showed up, and many kept coming. So we sat in the university chapel, facing the wall and thinking about nothing. In some ways it was much less impressive than the solemn meditation halls in Engakuji or Eiheiji, since we didn't have the setup to do the thing in style. Some used pillows and blankets in place of the beautiful little Zen cushion that is called a *zafu;* we didn't have the neat, straight-lined and disciplined atmosphere of the Zen temple; but then, needless to say, Western legs don't take easily to the lotus posture and the Western back tends to sag. Yet in spite of all this there was a hushed silence (latecomers sensed it instantly), a sense of union and an atmosphere of supernatural presence. Since some students complained that "just sitting" was somehow driving them into isolation, we began and ended with a good old hymn, "We are one in the Spirit, we are one in the Lord. . . ." Even to write about it gives me a pang of nostalgia for those happy days. It was, after all, a primitive endeavor, but it has convinced me that Zen in some shape or form has a future within Christianity. Western Christianity, I repeat, needs this kind of thing—the people are longing for it.

There was a little opposition, though less than I expected. I confess that I can understand the feelings of my critics. Conciliar ideas take some time to filter into the psychology of certain good people, and I saw at once that the recent influx of Oriental religions has perplexed not a few solid Christians in the California area. They don't know whether to thrust the whole damn business into the category of a Fellini-Satyricon end of the Roman Empire (an apocalyptic omen of the end of the West), or to welcome it with postconciliar comprehension, cooperation, and charity. I was not surprised, then, to find a few who looked on me as a Buddhist missionary out to topple the idols of Christianity. To a radically conservative Irish Catholic like myself, this was a little painful. Yet Irishmen gave me small support. I have always felt that my staunch fellow countrymen are among those less open to the gentle breeze of spirituality that blows from the Orient. They are more at home with "Hail, Glorious Saint Patrick" than with the lotus posture, and they look with alarm at the saffron robes, the beards, and the bare feet that speak of the esoteric East. Conversely, I found that if one wants to sell something like Zen, a guttural Teutonic accent pays better dividends than a brogue. This latter, in the United States, is more often associated with Irish coffee than with Oriental studies; and many people did not suppress their surprise and amusement at hearing an Irishman talking about Zen. Alas, in such circumstances what can one do but transcend the confines of time and space, entering into the serene air of pure nothingness?

Anyhow, since misunderstanding could arise, I thought it better to call the thing "Christian Zen" and make the business clear. Yet this was a bit embarrassing in view of the fact that I had just published a book in which I attacked all the talk about "Christian Zen" as being confusing. Now I was obliged to eat my words. Certainly the term will always be controversial, and some people won't like it. Nevertheless, after thinking the thing over again, I now am of the opinion that the term "Christian Zen" can be meaningful, provided one makes the necessary distinctions. Probably the strongest argument in its favor is the fact, already mentioned, that some of the Masters concede that Zen exists in Christianity. Perhaps they do not rate our brand as highly as their own—though even that is not certain—but they do recognize it. And if they recognize it, why not use the term? Anyhow, let me now recount briefly how I introduced the subject of Zen and how some people reacted.

First of all, I felt it necessary to distinguish between Zen and Zen Buddhism. This latter is a Buddhist sect which, it is said, originated in Canton in the sixth century A.D. when the Indian monk Bodhidharma, after sitting in meditation for nine years, finally obtained enlightenment. So long and with such determination did he sit facing the wall that his arms and legs fell off. And the little armless, legless statues of Dharma Sama can still be found all over Japan. Bodhidharma is a legendary figure, and scholars say that Zen originated from the confluence of Mahayana Buddhism and Taoism. Certainly marks of the Indian origin still remain in the vocabulary. The sanskrit *maya* becomes *makyo;* *dhyana* became *ch'an* in China and Zen in Japan; *samadhi* becomes *sanmai;* and so on. It is to the undying credit of Zen Buddhism, especially to the two great sects of Soto and Rinzai, to have preserved and developed Zen with such purity and severity. So much for Zen Buddhism.

The word Zen, on the other hand, means meditation, and that is why it need not be restricted to Buddhism. Not any old meditation at all, of course—not the discursive meditation wherein one reasons and thinks and makes resolutions. Rather is it a state of consciousness in which one sees into the essence of things; it extends throughout the day, so that one can say that Zen is walking, Zen is working, Zen is eating, Zen is life. It is meditation without an object. It is what elsewhere I have called "vertical meditation," because it is sometimes described as a "going down," a breaking through layers of consciousness to the depths of one's spirit or the core of one's being. One pays no attention to the thoughts and images that pass across the surface of the mind. One simply ignores them in favor of a deeper activity. In Christian

terms it may be better to call it contemplation rather than meditation, since it is so akin to the mental exercise described by the
great Christian contemplatives. This, like Zen, is sometimes
spoken of as darkness, emptiness, silence, nothingness. It has been
called "the dark night," not because it is particularly painful but
because of the absence of clear-cut thoughts and images in the
mind. Again, it is called the cloud of unknowing, because one is,
as it were, in a cloud without clear images and ideas. Sometimes
it is spoken of as "thinking of nothing"; but I like this terminology less because it can give rise to the misconception that Zen
or contemplation is a form of idling. A better term is "super-
thinking."

This meditation is existential in that it is not preoccupied with
past or future, right or left, up or down. One is simply in the
present (in the lotus posture one may have the feeling of being
locked there), in the eternal now, face to face with reality like
two mirrors. And all this may some day culminate in the trans-
forming experience known as *satori*. The bodily position is not
without importance, because Zen is meant to drive conviction
right down into the guts. Here it is in contrast with Western
prayer, which for the past couple of centuries has tended to be
very cerebral and has not rooted itself deeply in the personality,
with the result that many Christians, even nuns and priests, can
jettison long-held convictions in moments of emotional crisis.
Probably they would not be able to do this if their convictions
were lodged at the gut level through Zen.

This, more or less, was the way I explained the thing. Now it
has often been said that you cannot understand Zen unless you
do it and that there is no substitute for experience. This is probably true. And yet I found that the people I met got the idea
rather quickly, even before they actually sat. They got it much
more quickly than the people of a generation back. For the latter

all this talk about interior darkness and emptiness was so much rigmarole; and even spiritual writers were reluctant to write about it except for the initiated. They seemed to feel that they were dealing with an area of psychic life which could be sacred or diabolical and which, at all events, should be handled with delicacy. On the other hand, modern people are much more familiar with it all. Why?

One reason, I believe, is the widespread knowledge of psychoanalysis. Since the Freudian revolution people are acutely aware of their interior drives, subconscious anxieties, childhood fixations, archetypes, and all the rest. They are familiar with the description of the mind as an iceberg with only a fraction of its massive bulk protruding from the water. It is not hard for them to imagine depth upon depth in the mind, depths normally dormant until their powers of energy are released by something like Zen. When they are told about a meditation that penetrates through layers of consciousness to the very bottom, they somehow get an idea of what it's all about.

There is, I believe, a second reason why modern people get the hang of Zen rather easily, though I hesitate to mention it lest I be misunderstood. Anyhow, it is this: the widespread use of drugs. Now I am by no means advocating drugs. I have never experimented with them myself (perhaps I didn't have the courage), and am quite prepared to believe the horrendous things that are said about them. All I say here is that they seem to introduce people to a level of psychic life that has something in common with Zen and mysticism. I don't mean that the experience they induce is the same as Zen—it isn't, for it has altogether different effects—but similar psychological faculties seem to be brought into play. The result is that people who have used drugs understand a little about Zen, since they have been awakened to the realization that there is a depth in the mind worth exploring.

Not infrequently, I have been told, people begin with drugs and end up with Zen. Surely this is a consummation devoutly to be wished.

There were serious Christians who had difficulties about Zen. I don't mean prejudiced people, but others who were open but perplexed. Their problems, I believe, can be reduced to three.

First there was the whole problem of the place of God in Zen. I have already spoken of that and need not go into it again.

Secondly, there was the problem of the place of Christ in Zen. Some people felt that Christian Zen must be centered on Christ. And where was Christ in this void of imageless darkness? This is an important problem. I myself believe that Christian Zen can be Christ-centered, but I shall leave that to a later chapter.

The third problem can be dealt with here. Some asked: But how does Zen differ from "quietism"?

Quietism is one of these words that are bandied about by well-meaning people who don't quite know what they mean. If I understand it correctly, which is not certain, it is a form of idling that crept into contemplative prayer in the seventeenth century, taking the form of suppression of thought and activity. Undoubtedly it was a grotesque distortion of the real thing. And that similar distortions exist today when people are so anxious for kicks is beyond question. I suppose it is a matter that should be taken seriously, since it is certainly possible to sit in comfortable silence, enjoying a species of physical euphoria that has no religious significance whatever and makes nobody wiser than before.

But it should be remembered that Zen literature, no less than its Christian counterpart, is filled with anathemas against such things. "*Bonyari* Zen," which means "idling Zen," is roundly condemned by true Masters, who rightly insist that, far from idling, the true Zen demands a fantastic effort of mind and will and body. Thought is not just suppressed. As has been pointed out, the upper levels of consciousness are ignored in order that one may concentrate at a deeper level. Put in other words: one is not preoccupied with thought but with the ground of being from which thought takes its origin. Here lies the true self. Nor is there any question of just letting the mind run amuck. Deep down there is a concentration that is silent but intense; people practicing Zen are urged to use all their powers and energies to break through. And the key is the detachment that we have considered. In short, quietism could be a danger in Zen as in Christian contemplation; but, properly understood, Zen is not quietistic. Anyone who has been beaten by the stick or *kyosaku* knows this.

Again, if quietism means the negation of activity in such a way that one does no work, it is clear that no such charge can be leveled at Zen, which emphasizes work immensely. Indeed, to do one's work with total concentration and energy is one form of Zen practice and is a substitute for sitting in the meditation hall. This is frequently said by the Master.

Going further, it might be possible to define quietism in a broader sense. Then for Christians it would mean rest in anything that is not God. For Zen Buddhists it would mean rest in anything. And for practical purposes both are saying the same thing. The fact is that if you want to persevere to the end you must rest in nothing. Nothing, nothing, nothing, says John of the Cross, and on the mountain nothing. This means renunciation, not of alcohol and tobacco, but of all thoughts and desires (even thoughts and ideas of God), of all visions, sensible experiences, and the rest. The *Ascent of Mount Carmel* is a detailed catalogue of all things from which you must be detached, particularly those sweet spiritual experiences to which the mind cleaves. Unless a man renounces everything he possesses he cannot be my disciple. And everything means everything. How often people get attached to the joyful euphoria of their own *samadhi*; and they cling to it, they rest in it. And this, I believe, is a form of quietism that hinders progress. John of the Cross speaks of such attachments as the tiny thread around the foot of the bird, hindering it from soaring into the clear blue sky in serene freedom. A Buddhist author puts it in another way. A man is standing in the subway leaning on his umbrella when the train lurches. He must let go of the umbrella and grasp the rail—otherwise he is lost. So let go of your umbrella. Let it go. Don't cling to it or you'll fall flat on your face.

I write this to underline the radical nature of true mysticism, whether Buddhist or Christian. It is rest in nothing; it is no search for a beautiful experience or a thrilling kick. But let's remember, too, that renunciation is but one side of the picture. There is the treasure hidden in the field and the pearl of great price. To find these the suffering is worth while.

CHAPTER 5

CHRISTIAN ZEN (2)

I have tried to say that, on the admission of some Masters, Zen is found in religions other than Buddhism. If this is true, Zen ought already to exist in Christianity; and in that case the task of the Christian will be to find it, develop it, and make it relevant to our day with the help of the East. But where is Zen within the Christian tradition?

I confess that I would hate to go on record as stating that Zen is found in Christianity in exactly the same form as in Buddhism. This would be one of those simplified statements that drives everybody out of their mind, Christians and Buddhists alike, and I am not particularly anxious to lose all my friends. What I can safely say, however, is that there is a Christian *samadhi* that has always occupied an honored place in the spirituality of the West. This, I believe, is the thing that is nearest to Zen. It is this that I have called Christian Zen.

I have already spoken briefly about this *samadhi* which flourished in the great schools of spirituality that drove their roots into the rich cultural soil of medieval Europe. There were schools of Cistercians, Dominicans, Carmelites, Franciscans, and the rest. Then there were the Victorines—and schools of mysticism in the Rhineland and in Flanders and even in stolid old England. To say nothing of the great Orthodox schools that gave us the *Philokalia* and taught the prayer of the heart. All these schools had their way of leading to contemplative silence and peace,

beyond words, beyond images, beyond ideas, and beyond desire.
The contemplative experience went by various names. The author
of *The Cloud* describes it beautifully as "the blind stirring of
love." It is blind because it contains no thoughts and images,
being just like nothing; it is no more than a delicate and simple
interior movement of love in silence. Again, the same author
speaks of it as "the naked intent of the will." Mention of the will
indicates the element of love, while nakedness or nudity is traditionally used in Christian prayer to indicate complete detachment
from all things, even from thoughts and images and desires. "Be
sure that it be naked," the English author tells his disciple, and
he repeatedly warns him to be "unclothed" in his approach to
God. Other authors speak of it as the *silentium mysticum*, indicat-
ing that beyond all thought and speech there lies a realm of exquisite silence. Again, it is called "spiritual sleep" because it has a depth
and a quietness and a strength like that other beauty sleep which
is chief nourisher in life's great feast. John of the Cross (my
great guru) calls it "the living flame of love," referring to the
dynamic nature of this *samadhi*, which developing into a roaring
flame, comes to possess one's whole being and drives one on in
total self-forgetfulness. The same author refers to it as the dark
night because of the spiritual nudity or absence of thought that
characterizes the state of deep *samadhi*. The terminology stems
from a much earlier writer, Dionysius.

In the earnest practice of mystical contemplation, do thou leave behind the
senses and the working of the intellect, and all things that the senses and
the intellect can perceive, and all things which are not and all things that
are, and strain upwards in unknowing, as far as may be, to union with
Him who is above all things and above all knowledge. For by constant
and absolute withdrawal from thyself and all things in purity, abandon-

ing all and set free from all, thou shalt be carried up to the ray of Divine
darkness that surpasseth all being.*

This ray of divine darkness pierces brightly through the whole
apophatic school of mysticism of which John of the Cross is the
chief spokesman. His sister Teresa is less dark. For her, *samadhi*
is found at the center of the interior castle in the depth of one's
being. She refers to interior and spiritual senses of listening,
touching, and relishing, thus adding richness to the emptiness of
interior silence.

Each school had its own typical approach, but one thing common to all was an emphasis on love or divine charity. Here, of
course, the basic intuition comes from the Scriptures, particularly
from the text which states that he who loves knows God and he
who does not love does not know God. Enlightenment was the
fruit of love, which was like a candle that gives light and enables
one to see. "Proffer thy candle to the flame," writes the author of
The Cloud, asking us to enlighten our hearts from the immense
flame that is the love of God. Somehow love drives people down
to the psychic level where *samadhi* is found (and I believe this
is true also of human love) and wisdom is relished. For contemplation itself was not precisely love, but wisdom—the beautiful
sapientia that medieval Christianity esteemed so much. "If anyone loves me he will be loved of my Father and we will send the
Spirit . . . ." The spirit of wisdom was given to those who love.

In the technique of introducing people to *samadhi*, the Western tradition differed considerably from Zen. There was no lotus
position and little about bodily posture. There does seem to have
been considerable interest in breathing, particularly in the Eastern Church and in the tradition that flourished around Mount

*My own translation.

Athos, but much of this was lost or forgotten, and the farther West one moves the more cerebral the whole thing becomes. People were introduced to meditation by reading the Scriptures and reflection on their contents. Gradually this discursive meditation would develop into something more simplified (like the repetition of an aspiration or word), and eventually into the wordless and supraconceptual silence which is contemplation—or, if you prefer the word, Christian *samadhi*. This was a stage at which everyone seriously devoted to mental prayer should arrive. It was the ordinary development of meditation.

This is the way I was taught to meditate when I entered the novitiate (or joined the party) somewhere out in the bog. I was told to take the Bible, or some book about the Bible, and to chew and ruminate and digest and pray. For a start, this was pretty good, and I would recommend anyone to begin in this way. My only complaint is that in religious orders at that time, and now also, nothing further was taught. The old medieval tradition of leading people through various stages to *samadhi* was more or less lost. It just was not customary to introduce people to supraconceptual forms of prayer; and as for "mysticism," this was not a good word. Needless to say, if people stumbled on *samadhi* or got there under their own steam, as many did, there was nothing to stop them, but skilled direction and efficient methodology was greatly lacking.

Aldous Huxley and others have blamed the Jesuits for the decline in mysticism in nineteenth-century Europe, accusing the sons of Ignatius of teaching a species of prayer that was more like mathematics than contemplation. But perhaps this is not entirely fair. Other factors were at work. For one thing, a healthy reticence about mysticism was considered prudent in view of the wave of false mysticism that had wrought havoc in religious life at an earlier period. Then there was the spirit of the times (what my German friends, if I hear them correctly, call the *Zeitgeist*), which always hits monasteries hard—as the permissive society hits them hard today. In the last century it was a spirit of scientism, of rationalism, of dogmatism that esteemed concepts, images, mathematics, ideas, and was quite bewildered by the silent darkness of mystical wisdom. All this militated against the mystical tradition. Add to it the general decline of Western stamina in the last decade and you understand why so many religious orders have lost their mysticism, and with it their vision.

It is just at this juncture that Zen and other forms of Oriental mysticism appear on the horizon. I believe they have something to say to us. I believe they can help the tottering religious orders to rethink some problems and to make some changes. And they can also help the Christian layman to enter into *samadhi*. Faced with this phenomenon from the East, however, and anxious to learn from the Oriental treasure house, the Westerner can adopt either of two attitudes.

First, he can jettison his own tradition to become all Oriental. Neglecting the great giants of his past, he can sit at the feet of the *roshi* and endeavor to obtain a *satori* that has been handed down through many generations from the time of Bodhidharma and even from the time of the Buddha. In this way he stands in the full stream of Eastern Buddhism, and if he is a Christian he can take his *satori* into a Christian framework. Some Western people have taken this line.

I myself, however, could never do things in this way. Perhaps Jung and Eliot have made me feel too deeply the power of tradition and the strength of those archetypes that are lodged down deep within me. Jung was enthusiastic about Zen and yoga; but he insisted that in their Eastern form they do not suit Western man, who has a different tradition and different archetypes. In a famous sentence he said that the West would have its own yoga, built upon the foundations of Christianity. Here, I believe, he had a charismatic flash of prophecy, uttering words that will soon be fulfilled. Together with Jung, Eliot keeps telling us that the past is present—that it is living in us, part of us, pushing us on. If this is so, is it possible to cast away one's past and substitute another? Is it possible to throw out Western archetypes and replace them with those of the East? For me it is not. And in spite of having lived in the East for twenty years, in spite of loving Japan very deeply, I still feel incorrigibly Western and even, *alas,* incorrigibly Irish. Obviously this is not to say that my own tradition is superior—I don't believe it is—but simply that it is a fact.

For this reason it has always seemed to me that the psychologically realistic way of doing things is to stand in the stream of one's own tradition and humbly take what is good and valuable from another. In particular it is the work of the great religious orders—Dominicans, Franciscans, Jesuits, and so on—to rediscover the mystical tradition they have lost and enrich it with the spiritual insights that the East has to offer. This may mean forgoing the apostolic joy of teaching mathematics, walking in demonstrations, and running bazaars. But the sacrifice would surely be worth while.

About this blood transfusion—learning what we can and integrating it with our past—I have already said something in an earlier chapter. Now let me add a few more words. How can Zen update and make relevant the tradition of Christian contemplation that goes back for more than a millennium and is now in dire need of renewal? First of all, I think that things like Zen can help us update and demythologize much of the theology that underlies Christian mysticism. Let me explain what I mean.

The Judaeo-Christian tradition, as is well known, is extremely theocentric. Everything hinges on God. This stems in large measure from the Bible, where all is attributed to the guiding hand of Yahweh. If the rain falls, this is the work of Yahweh. If someone goes astray, Yahweh hardens his heart. If he dies, Yahweh strikes him down. And so on. This is all the more stressed in the communication of God to man: the great experiences of Abraham, Moses, and Paul had nothing whatever to do with their own efforts, their own asceticism, their own prayer. All was the gift of Yahweh. This was carried over into the Christian mystical tradition, where everything was the work of God and the activity of man received little attention. What I have called Christian *samadhi* went by the name of infused contemplation because it was a pure gift poured into the soul by God alone.

Now this is a legitimate way of speaking. Ultimately it is very true, and the Hebrew was right in attributing everything to God. But it has the disadvantage of making people lazy in developing the human faculties that make for mysticism. It has the further disadvantage of being rather unacceptable to modern man, who is extremely anthropocentric and has difficulty with a terminology that incessantly (and to him needlessly) keeps harping on God. He has demythologized the action of God in the natural sphere by finding all kinds of secondary causes, and he finds difficulty with a Christian mystical theory which clings constantly to the direct action of God and is stubbornly theocentric.

As opposed to this, Zen is extremely man-centered and existential. You are simply told to sit and get on with the job. The instructions are concerned with your spine and your eyes and your abdomen; in a very practical way you are led to *samadhi* without too much theory. What you are asked to believe is that you possess the Buddha nature and that enlightenment is possible.

Here is something for Christianity. Terminology about acquired and infused contemplation, about ordinary and extraordinary prayer, about *gratia gratis data* and *gratia gratum faciens*—all these complications can quietly and conveniently be dropped. They aren't really necessary, because the experience itself is frightfully simple and uncomplicated. In my opinion we could even dispense with the word contemplation and put in its place "Christian *samadhi*." This would have the good effect of bringing us into line with other spiritual traditions which use this word. Besides, contemplation is a Latin word, translation of the Greek *theoria*. Must Christians forever stick to the Hellenistic vocabulary?

By using a language that people understand and employing a technique they can practice, it should be possible to introduce a great number of people to Christian *samadhi*. This would be an enormous boon to Christianity—particularly to Catholic Christianity, which finds its people losing interest in the rosary, the way of the Cross, novenas, and all the devotions that have propped up the popular faith in the past. If these go, and mind you I'm not saying they should, their place may be taken by a simple contemplation accessible to anyone with good will. The old Christian contemplation was for an elite—it was for Franciscans, Jesuits, Dominicans, and the good people I have spoken about. But the poor layman, a second-class citizen, was left with his beads. It need no longer be so. Just as the liturgy has broadened out to embrace everyone, so contemplation can broaden out too. The wretched wall that divided popular Christianity from monastic Christianity can be broken down so that all may have vision, all may reach *samadhi*.

Nor is this to say that the role of the poor Franciscans, the wise Dominicans, the wily Jesuits, and the rest has come to a happy end. No, these should be contemplatives by profession, leaders of the rest. In this way they can do a great service to the community and to the world. But if they persist in doing things that the world can do better, they will simply cease to exist. They will have no reason for existence and little relevance for society. Others will take their place.

CHAPTER 6

CHRIST

Speaking about Zen to Christians I have found myself faced with the wide-eyed question, "But what about Christ? How does Christ fit into this void, this emptiness, this darkness that transcends thought?"

This is an obvious and inescapable question. Anybody with even a kindergarten grasp of Christianity knows that Christ is the center of the whole business and that to exclude Christ would be the prime sellout. Naturally, then, people are wary of a Christian prayer that seems to put aside the Scriptures (no dependence on words and letters) and excludes thoughts and images of Christ in order to enter into the darkness of nothing. And needless to say, all this is a pretty formidable challenge to anybody foolish enough to start gabbing about Christian Zen.

I myself believe that if Christian Zen is to be Christian and not simply Zen, it must be somehow Christocentric and somehow built on the Scriptures. But I ask myself if through Zen we may not find a new approach to Christ, an approach that is less dualistic and more Oriental. This statement may sound strange (if anything sounds strange in the crazy modern Church), but I believe that it is pretty reasonable.

Let me go back to something I tried to say earlier. Dialogue does not simply mean that Buddhists and Christians sit around sipping green tea and exchanging pleasantries in a palsy-walsy atmosphere of ecumenical good will. It means that they settle down and learn something from one another. They get new ideas, new attitudes, new insights. And it is this I am talking about now: from Buddhism we can get new insights into our approach to Christ.

We ought to be open to this kind of thing, because it is what our forebears did. Christianity, after all, began as a Jewish thing, but Augustine, Gregory, and the rest did not swallow the whole bit, hook, line, and sinker as it came from Judaism. These men lived in a Greek culture; they carried Greek insights into the Jewish revelation, and so Christianity grew and was enriched. Now if Augustine and Gregory did not take the whole thing from the Jews, I can't see why the Orientals should take it hook, line, and sinker from us. They will have their own insights, their own attitudes—and they will add a lot to Christianity, just as Greek culture added a lot.

That is what I mean by saying that if we go to Christ through Zen we find him in a different way from the person who goes to him through Aristotle. I love that passage in Second Corinthians where Paul speaks of the glory of God in the face of Moses and the glory of God in the face of Jesus. What radiant brightness and divine power is there! And do we little Westerners think we have seen all that glory? Do we claim to have exhausted all that beauty? Do we imagine we have explored all that wisdom? Far from it. In the face of Christ are myriads of contours yet to be explored; his voice speaks in rich and vibrant tones that Western ears have never heard; his eyes are pools of wisdom the Western gaze has never fathomed. And now it is the hour of the East to explore all this beauty and find what the West has missed. What an exciting adventure! But let me, a mere foreign barbarian who has spent twenty years in the mystic East, attempt to stammer some words about this new approach to the glory of God in the face of Jesus.

Once in a Buddhist temple I heard a good old *roshi* deliver a talk on detachment from words and ideas. Words, he said, using a traditional Buddhist simile, are like a finger pointing to the moon. Cling to the finger and you'll never see the moon. This I felt to be eminently reasonable and true. Words, any words, even the words of Scripture, are fingers that point to something else. As long as we cling to words we will never have real vision.

And, of course, Western man loves his little words and clings to them like a child clutching his favorite toy. He clings to his concepts, images, figures, adding machines, and computers, forgetting that all these things are fingers pointing to the moon. Today his main problem is that he has got enmeshed and fouled up in mass communications and the secular city, forgetting again that these are no more than pointing fingers. Transferring this attitude to the Scriptures, he clings to the words and the phrases, and he is in danger of adoring images and concepts of God instead of God himself. A strange form of idolatry.

What I am getting at here is that words and concepts and images of Christ are not Christ. Let us at least reflect on the possibility that Christ can be known without ideas—that he can be known in the darkness, in the void, in the emptiness that transcends thought. The Scriptures are the finger (and we need the Scriptures just as we need the finger), but Christ is the moon. Let us not get so involved with fingers that we miss the moon.

Or take something else from Zen. Anybody who has dabbled a little in Suzuki and the others has heard the famous dictum: "If you meet the Buddha, slay him!" This is often taken as a blasphemous rejection of all that is religious or sacred—sometimes as proof that Zen holds nothing sacrosanct, even the Buddha.

But I do not read it this way. I prefer the interpretation that says, "If you see the Buddha, what you see is not the Buddha. So slay him!" The underlying idea is not unlike the finger and the moon. Anything—absolutely anything—that you see or hear or touch is not the genuine article. Kill it! It is no more than the finger pointing to the moon. It may be very precious; but if your right hand scandalizes you, cut it off.

Now I believe that there is something for Christians here. Properly and piously understood, one can say, "If you meet Christ, slay him!" And the meaning is: "What you see is not Christ."

The slaying metaphor, of course, is pretty grim and overstates the problem. Because, as I have said, concepts and images and pictures are as necessary as the finger, and it's not a good idea to do away with them altogether. On the other hand, the slay-the-Buddha motif is meant as practical direction for time of meditation. Get rid of the Buddha as an object of thought, it means, if you want to realize your Buddha nature. And in the same way one can say, get rid of images of Christ if you want the high contemplative union with Christ which is the real thing.

In short, what it comes to is this. It is not necessary to have clear-cut images and concepts of Christ. If you have no such concepts you may be in the stage where you have forgotten about the finger, fascinated by the pale and tranquil beauty of the autumn moon. And if so, how happy you are! You have left the dirty cave of Plato and are out in the beautiful sunlit air. Don't let these grubby little merchants drag you back to the murky underworld of conceptualization. Stay out. Enjoy your *samadhi*. Christ is with you.

Now I can immediately envisage some of my readers considering this a lot of nonsense. They will say that we can, in fact, have an image of Christ; we can have a picture of the eternal Galilean who dominates Matthew, Mark, Luke, and John. After all, have we not his portrait? So how can you throw images and concepts out the window as if they were so much garbage. And to this I

would answer again that concepts are not trash but the finger
pointing to the moon.

   Christ is the moon because the men who wrote the gospel are
leading their reader to a vision not only of the historical Jesus
(of whom we assuredly can have concepts) but of the risen
Christ, the cosmic Christ, the Christ who was at the beginning.
And it is he who escapes all images, all thoughts, all ideas, and all
pictures. The risen Christ is so far beyond concepts that we find
Paul struggling with all kinds of words to express the inexpressible. Here is Paul on Jesus.

> His is the primacy over all created things
>   For in him were created
>   All things in heaven and on earth;
> Everything visible and everything invisible
> Thrones, dominations, sovereignties, powers,
> All things were created through him and for him.
> Before everything was created he existed
>   And he holds all things in unity.

   Don't let anyone tell me that Paul is here speaking about some
simple reality that can be expressed in concepts and images! Nor
is he speaking of Jesus just as he was in his earthly, preresurrec-
tion form. For Paul, Christ is a "secret" or a "mystery" or whatever you want to call it, and he keeps pointing one finger after
another at the moon that no human eye can descry. The poor
scholars get all tied up in Paul's fingers; the mystics turn toward
the moon.

   The living and risen Christ of Paul who is with men all days is
the unknowable Christ, coextensive with the universe and buried
in the hollow recesses of the human heart. The deepest thing in
Paul is not Paul but Christ. It is not Paul who lives, but Christ

who lives in him. It is not Paul who cries out "Abba, Father," it is the spirit of Christ within who utters this cry. For Paul, to live is Christ and to die is Christ—and it is all the same. If this is true for Paul, it is true for anyone who believes. The deepest thing within him is not himself but Christ.

I believe that Paul is trying to say something like this to the Ephesians when he makes the prayer, "that Christ may dwell by faith in your hearts." The word "heart" here is a direct translation of the Greek; but Paul, a Jew born and bred, probably had in mind the Hebrew word, which means the core of being, the deepest self. So for Paul, Christ is beyond concepts, beyond images, beyond thought, beyond place. If we want to situate him anywhere, we should situate him where thought takes its origin, because he is our original face before we were born. That is why Paul can say that we were chosen in Christ before the foundation of the world.

One step further. If Christ is deep, deep down at the center of reality and in the depths of the heart—if he is somehow like the true self, then there will be times when we do not know him reflectively. This is because there is no I-Thou relationship any longer. It is of the very nature of the deepest realms of our psyche to move, urge on, inspire, and direct without being known in a subject-object way—the charity of Christ drives us on, says Paul. Nor is it only Paul. Luke tells us how Jesus warned his disciples not to think too much when they were dragged before princes and kings.

"Keep this carefully in mind: you are not to prepare your defence because I myself will give you an eloquence and a wisdom that none of your opponents will be able to resist or contradict" (Luke 21). Face to face with the judge or the hangman, one shouldn't start asking, "What would Jesus do now?" No, get rid of all this dualistic stuff. Because the answer is going to come from your very guts where the deepest thing lies. Here Jesus and Zen are together. No reasoning. No reflection. The answer is going to come from a part of your being that you scarcely know exists.

I have talked about Paul and said a word about Luke; but John is just the same. The great John, the beloved disciple—what a fantastic sense he had of the glory of Jesus! "We have seen his glory . . . ." And for him Jesus was the "true" everything, the Greek *alethinos*. Jesus is the true vine, the true bridegroom, the true way, the true life, the truth itself. He is the genuine vine, and other vines that we see are second-class imitations of the real product. Here is another poetic way of speaking about the cosmic dimensions of a risen Christ who is at the center of all that is. "And I, if I be lifted up from the earth will draw all things to myself."

Of course when I talk about the cosmic Christ I want to maintain some balance, which is not easy in a world that is topsy-turvy and upside down. I mean that some theologians in their zest for the living Christ tend to cut the link between the cosmic Christ and the historical Christ. No doubt they feel that this is a felicitous, ecumenical virtue, since if the cosmic Christ is divorced from the historical Christ, the cosmic Christ can be equated with the all-pervading Buddha nature, and everyone feels happy in sweet, ecumenical unanimity. But alas, things are not so easy, and neither true Buddhists nor true Christians feel happy when things are ironed out in this way. If one has a minimum of fidelity to Paul and John and Luke and the rest, one sees that the cosmic Christ is precisely the Jesus who shed his blood. If anything is clear in the preaching of the New Testament, it is the fact that the once crucified Jesus is now alive—even the wildest exegetes cannot find in the Bible a discontinuity between Jesus of Nazareth and the Christ who has the primacy over all things. I want to stress this in parenthesis lest I be identified with a lot of gnostic rubbish that creates air pollution in the theological skies of our day.

Returning, however, to the cosmic dimensions of Christ who is at the deepest heart of man, this is something that can have enormous repercussions on the life of meditation for the Christian. It means that meditation need not be confined to the I-Thou brand that has been the warp and woof of popular Christian prayer. Not that the I-Thou approach is excluded. It must always be there. But it is not the whole story. Let me try, then, to sketch briefly a Christocentric path of Zen meditation.

The starting point will be the Scriptures, which should be read or heard or experienced in liturgy. This is the indispensable groundwork without which no Christian meditation can exist. And if we have Christian Zen meditation halls (as I hope we soon will) I believe that the air should be pervaded with Scripture and liturgy and the atmosphere of faith, without which the void might well become a literal void and not the rich fullness of mystical emptiness. Furthermore, in the early stages, meditation (particularly in the case of Western people) may be dualistic, or rationalistic, or whatever you want to call this reflection and dialogue with God that is traditionally central to Christian prayer. Paul began in a dualistic way. He began with a conversation with Christ on the road to Damascus, and the I-Thou approach seems to continue in *Philippians*, where he is running after Christ like an athlete in the Isthmian games. If a Christian, too, wants to start in the footsteps of Paul, running after Christ—well, this is all right. But if he wants to go on to anything like Zen, the thinking process must simplify, the words must decrease, the dualism must give way to the void of emptiness which is the *silentium mysticum*. Now he is doing something like Zen—*gedo* Zen, perhaps, but still Zen. He is getting away from the finger and

beginning to look toward the moon. He cannot see the moon
(for it is beyond the cloud of unknowing) but he is drawn to it
even so, and he does not want to be bothered with pious reflec-
tions about the finger. He does not want to be ensnared even by its
delicate silken beauty and its white-skinned softness. Its very
beauty may be a temptation now, distracting him from the quiet
splendor of the moon. It is the finger of enlightened men—Matthew, Mark, Luke, and John—who saw something and want
their readers to see it too. "These things I have written in order
that you may believe." So let him forget the finger and, without
any solicitude whatever, look quietly toward the silent beauty
of that hidden moon. He may find, in Paul's masterly phrase, that
his life is hidden with Christ in God. His self is hidden, Christ is
hidden, and only God remains. (Shades again of my old *roshi*.)
But if this is you, remember that you will be there, very much
alive; Christ is there, very much alive; but you are not conscious
of yourself or of Christ—because your life is hidden with Christ
in God. Eventually enlightenment will come. Not any enlightenment, but the one toward which the finger points. Abba, Father!

CHAPTER 7

KOAN

People sometimes say that Zen is crazy and that anyone interested in the business should have his, or her, head examined. It's
not my intention here to refute or substantiate this accusation,
since, apart from everything else, protestations of personal sanity
don't convince anyone anyhow. What I want to do is to discuss
the *koan*, which is one of the seemingly crazy elements in Zen.

Koan literally means "a public document," but as used in Zen
it has absolutely nothing to do with public documents (here we
go on the first happy spree of irrationalities) and simply means
a paradoxical problem. It is a problem that is kept before the
mind's eye or, more correctly, held in the pit of the belly, not
only in time of *zazen* but at all times, day in and day out, until
one eventually breaks through to enlightenment. The *koan* is not
solved by reason—it defies all logic—but by a process of identi-
fication. One lives the thing, forgets self, and in the end forgets
the *koan* also. Zen is full of amusing anecdotes about people
struggling and wrestling with *koan*. And then there is the story of
the monk who, having solved his *koan*, slapped his poor old *roshi*
on the face as if to say, "There now! I'm as good as you."

Here are some examples of *koan*.

What was the shape of your original face before you were
born?

57

or

We know the sound of two hands clapping,
But what is the sound of one hand clapping?

or

Mu (Nothing)

Meditation on these paradoxes often begets great anguish until
one breaks through to the joyful solution—which has nothing to
do with logic and is utterly bewildering to the uninitiated. Here
are some Zen questions and answers.

A monk asked Tung-shan, "Who is the Buddha?"
"Three *chin* of flax," came the answer.

or

A monk asked Chao-chou, "What is the meaning of the first
patriarch's visit to China?"
"The cypress tree in the front courtyard," came the answer.

The *koan* has attracted the attention of not a few Westerners
today. Perhaps this is because the cult of wisdom within the
irrational has been in vogue for some decades and is still on the
upswing. I can't help feeling that a little of this is due to my
fellow countryman James Joyce, whose later writing is full of
strange things that sound like *koan*. Perhaps it is no accident that
Joyce is popular in Japan, and that not a few Japanese professors,
visiting Ireland, have gone to Clongowes to gaze pensively at
the spot where the great man suffered at the hands of his vicious
persecutors. I myself don't fall down in admiration before Joyce

and consider him something of a nut or something of a leg-puller. For this reason I have been embarrassed to hear Japanese people say to me, "Irish? Oh, James Joyce!" Yet Joyce, even if a nut, is an interesting nut; and I suppose that in my heart of hearts, if the truth were known, I am proud of his stupid *koan* (though I shouldn't call them *koan* because they aren't) in *Ulysses* and *Finnegans Wake*. I suppose he liked a leg-pull and laughed at the solemnity of his scholarly interpreters. This, however, is a temptation of all *koan*-makers and I suspect (though here I may be wrong) that even good old Dr. Suzuki enjoyed a leg-pull from time to time.

Be that as it may, the *koan* is a baffling business. At one time I thought it was a gimmick to frustrate the mind at its upper level of discursive reasoning, thus forcing it to break through to a deeper level of psychic activity. I still think that this is one of its functions, and I believe I got a tiny glimmer of insight into it when I visited Expo '70 in Osaka. I was on my way to the south of Japan and took the opportunity to jump off the fast train and spend a few hours looking around that vast complex of glittering exhibitions from the countries of the world. What impressed me was the psychedelic dimension of the whole thing. The shrieking music, the flashing colors, the revolving screens, the wild designs, and all the rest. I wondered what wise old Aristotle would make of it all if he had the chance to toddle through this Babylon in his ragged old toga or whatever he wore. Would he have decided to add another chapter to the *Metaphysics*? Or would he in consternation have screamed for help to those pretty Japanese hostesses floating delicately around the place and flooding the air with smiling Oriental charm? What I mean is that there was little there to appeal to the discursive intellect with which Aristotle penetrated the earth and the stars. I saw at once that there was no use asking, "What does it all mean?" That was simply the wrong approach. I must go in, not to understand but to get the experience—to get the kick. This I did and found Expo '70 enthralling. I didn't scream to the pretty hostesses, but I added a chapter to my metaphysics.

Now I don't mean precisely that Expo '70 was one big *koan*, but to my mind it was something like that. And now I see that the *koan* contains an element of psychedelic wisdom that the discursive intellect (which I always foist off on poor Aristotle) cannot grasp. To get the hang of the *koan* you have to walk into it as I walked into Expo '70. You have to identify with it, live it. Since it is filled with paradox, it is filled with the anguish of life and the contradiction of existence. It is only by living through this terrible suffering of anguished contradiction that you can overcome the dispersion of dualism and reach the joy of enlightenment. If you look carefully at the *koan* you can see that they usually lead to unification or what we call (erroneously, I think) monism. For example, "the sound of one hand clapping" is obviously leading away from dispersion to unity. The *koan* may also, on the other hand, lead you down to the center of your being, to the core of your existence. "The shape of your original face" is clearly leading to the depth of the mind, to the place from which all thought takes its origin. One is being led to the source from which thought bubbles up. This is the original face. This is "the big self."

But, I repeat, one cannot get there by discursive reasoning and thinking or by playing around with syllogisms. This wisdom can only be grasped by deeper faculties that are normally dormant, particularly dormant in a generation that has blunted its sensibilities with radio, television, orange juice, and steaks. The *koan* gets these things out of one's system, triggering the mystical faculties into action and opening up a new level of topsy-turvy psychedelic wisdom that we all possess without knowing it. To

get those mystical faculties cracking we have to clear the mind of
the trash that we collect in modern living and then focus it on
something else. The *koan* has this effect; it purifies and leads to
wisdom. Probably it has more in common with art than with
philosophy or science. True art, as Eliot or someone said, can
communicate before it is understood—a statement which is certainly true of *The Waste Land*. Here is a poem that has com-
municated to all kinds of people, but if anyone knows what it's
all about I would like to meet him and sit at his feet. I have
read the poem several times with my students. We enjoyed it
immensely (and perhaps even got a shred of communal enlightenment), but we didn't understand so very much. I began to see
what the critics mean when they say that art does not mean; it
is. The same might be said of the *koan*. It does not mean; it is.
It lives the contradiction and the anguish and the absurdity of
existence.

Now I have often asked myself if all this has any relevance
for modern Christianity. At one time I thought it had none, and
this was the opinion of my colleagues also. We just didn't get
the hang of it all. Perhaps this was partly due to an education
that saw primarily the order and harmony of a universe proclaiming the existence of a divine artist, and only secondarily the
disorder, the anguish, the contradiction, and the pain—all that
we call the problem of suffering. Be that as it may, not being able
to handle the *koan*, we decided to give it a wide berth. We
avoided *Rinzai Zen*, which puts great emphasis on the *koan*
exercise, and directed our attention to *Soto Zen*, which inclines
more to *shikan taza*, meaning "just sitting." Now, however, I
have changed my mind (I do that fairly often) and have come to
the conclusion that the *koan* approach contains something of
tremendous value. I see it as a help to the understanding of our
Christian Scriptures and as a guide to a meditation based upon

biblical paradox. But is there anything vaguely corresponding to the *koan* in the Christian Scriptures?

It seems to me that Paul was one of the great *koan*-makers of all time, and it takes a pretty enlightened person to get what he's at. Take, for instance, the beginning of First Corinthians. Here Paul makes it clear that Christ crucified is utterly crazy to Jew and Gentile alike; but once you get enlightened, he is the truest wisdom. And this is the *koan*, something that looks crazy but isn't. I believe that the Christian who stares at the crucifix for hours and hours (and how many have done just that!) is face to face with a heart-rending *koan*. What confronts him is not only the absurdity of a crucified God, but the absurdity of his own suffering and the suffering of mankind. The whole thing is absurd, and it is epitomized in this twisted, crucified figure. So one does not try to understand by reasoning and thinking. One simply identifies with it, living the anguish, living the suffering; and eventually, after hours of wrestling with the crucifix, one may break through to the enlightenment of seeing sense in what looks like nonsense. Then comes resurrection. One has found unity in the terrible dispersion of a suffering Christ.

Taken in this way, the famous "Jesus prayer" of the Hesychasts, in which the word Jesus is recited rhythmically with the breathing, can be a *koan*. For in Jesus are summed up all the contradictions and sufferings and anxieties of man as such. He is a great archetypal figure, set for the rise and the fall of many; he is the sign that is to be contradicted. By living death with him, one breaks through to resurrection and a Jesus enlightenment.

Nor is all this so far from Buddhism as might appear at first sight. A student of Theravada Buddhism once told me that she had asked her old Master the question, "What type of person is the perfectly enlightened man? What would he be like?"

And to her shocked surprise, the Master retorted, "He would be despised, laughed at, and scorned by everyone." The crucified, the servant of Yahweh, the murdered Socrates, the despised *roshi*. Don't they all form part of the big contradictory picture of malicious stupidity and martyred goodness which is the *koan* history of poor mankind?

The Gospels, too, abound in *koan*. All this talk about plucking out your eye and cutting off your hand and what not. And then:

Let the dead bury their dead and come, follow me!

or

He that loves his life will lose it.

or

I am the vine and you are the branches.

or

This is my body.

Will anyone doubt that this goes beyond reason? Will anyone say that it is less baffling than Zen? I believe it could be argued that any religion demanding faith has its *koan*. Perhaps it could be argued that Christianity is one tremendous *koan* that makes the mind boggle and gasp in astonishment; and faith is the breakthrough into that deep realm of the soul which accepts paradox and mystery with humility. Quite certainly there were points in which Jesus makes it clear that he is talking in *koan* that defy explanation. Take celibacy. He that has ears to hear, let him hear. As if to say, if you don't understand, I can't help you—not, at any rate, at the level of discursive thinking.

All this makes me think that the *koan* opens up for Christians a new, yet old, approach to their Scriptures. I was set thinking along these lines by the remark of a Buddhist monk to a Christian friend of mine to the effect that Christians would get enlightenment if only they knew how to read their own Scriptures. I thought it rather big of him to say this, to admit so clearly that the Christian Scriptures contain enlightenment for the reader capable of getting it.

So let us use the Scriptures as *koan*. We need this to counterbalance the academic approach to the Bible that has characterized the last century. I mean that wise scholars have deciphered old languages, dug up pots in the desert, discovered musty manuscripts in dark caves, and unearthed ancient cities; and this has sometimes led them to the bright conclusion that they have plumbed the depth of biblical wisdom. But however valuable their pots and manuscripts (and they are valuable, very valuable), they don't help you solve the *koan* that flash out and hit you from the pages of the Scriptures. The old, old doctrine on which à Kempis and company went to town was that unless the Spirit speaks from within, you cannot really understand. This is what I mean when I say (in language that is a little demythologized) that the discursive faculties don't get a message that is grasped only by the deeper mystical faculties operating where the Spirit speaks to man.

So I suggest that you read the Scriptures as *koan*. Walk into them as you might walk into the psychedelic glory of Expo '70. Put aside for a while your critical faculties of reasoning and arguing. Stop asking whether Jesus did or did not walk on the waters, whether there was or was not a star to guide the Wise Men. Stop asking what it all means; because what it means is

less important than what it does to you. Forget all the complications and let the words enter the visceral area of your body,
where they will finely and delicately begin to act, to live, to
change you. Let the words of Scripture enter into you like the
body and blood of Christ to give you warmth and love and life.
Let them live at the psychedelic level. Get the kick those Semitic
writers are trying to give you. Then you'll find that the Scriptures are food and that they are life.

Doing this, you'll be in good company, because that is the
way Matthew, Mark, Luke, and John frequently read the Old
Testament. By standards of modern scholarly criticism, these
four men were idiots. They turn the Old Testament upside down,
applying to Jesus Old Testament words and phrases that no self-
respecting scholar in his wildest dreams would use in this way.
Jesus himself played fast and loose with the Old Testament.
"If you believed in Moses you would believe me—for he spoke
of me." I wonder what scholar would agree that Moses was
talking about Jesus. You can't believe that Moses spoke of Jesus
unless you read the Old Testament with psychedelic eyes as
the mystics read it.

Yes, the mystics. The handling of Scripture by John of the
Cross, Bernard, and the rest is absurd to the scholar, who smiles
patronizingly at their psychedelic dreams. But is it not simply
that the mystic has a different approach? He is using different
faculties; he is speaking not from the head but from the breast
or from the guts; he is speaking from a realm that lies beyond
and beneath the superficial discursiveness of the scholar. Yet
he is grasping a true message, because the men who wrote the
Scriptures were operating at this level. They were *koan*-makers
who did not write for scientists and did not want to be taken at
the level of rationalization alone.

One more interesting point about the *koan*. Once you solve

one, you can solve many. Months of wrestling with the first lead
to great facility in running through others. This is because the
deep mystical faculties have been opened up by the first break-
through and now they are in action—now you are capable of
identifying with the *koan*. And the same holds true for the Bible.
Break-through in one passage leads to enlightenment, joy, and
enthusiasm in reading the rest. Understanding Paul opens one's
faculties to the *Apocalypse* and to *Job*. In the Zen tradition, one
test of the validity of an enlightenment is the ability to solve
the *koan*. No real Master will tell you that you are enlightened
simply because you have blown your head off with a seemingly
big *satori*. Instead, he may ask you to solve a *koan*, and here is
the real test. In the same way, the test of an enlightened Christian could be his ability to read the Scriptures with joy, relish,
élan, and insight. If he can do this, the chances are that he has
had something like enlightenment somewhere along the line,
whether he realizes it or not. Somehow, somewhere he has heard
the voice of the fair Lady Wisdom who calls out in the streets
and raises her voice in the market place. He has consorted with
her and he is happy.

Coming to the practical aspect of meditation, if a Christian
wants to use the *koan* exercise, let him select from the Bible a
koan that appeals to him and keep it constantly by him, with
faith that it contains enlightenment and that a break-through
is possible. I have suggested the crucifix as a *koan*, or the word
"Jesus." But others are possible. Just as Zen uses the *koan Mu*, so
a Christian can use the *koan* God. The author of *The Cloud*
suggests words like "love" or "sin" for use in meditation; these
too could be *koan*.

Finally I would like to protest that in all this I am not glorifying
the cult of irrationality, nor do I want to be anti-intellectual. I
believe in reason, and in *The Still Point* I spent a whole chapter

trying to prove that the seeming irrationality of the mystics is consonant with reason. Perhaps those pages are not altogether successful, but I would like them accepted as evidence of good will. What I want to say here is that there is more in the Scriptures than words, and that the euphoric joy of digging up pots in the desert should not blind us to the existence of spirit and life. The *koan* exercise may teach us to see into the essence of the Scriptures. Perhaps it is a star from the East, standing in the sky and showing us the place where the child is with his mother.

CHAPTER 8

THE BODY

Anyone interested in meditation has to think about the body, because Brother Ass just won't let himself be ignored. There are few areas of human experience where the interaction of mind and matter is so important and yet so delicate as here. Perhaps Paul himself experienced this. Whether he was in the body or out of the body he just didn't know—God alone knew.

When you come to Oriental religions the attention paid to the body is striking. It is with the body that the whole thing begins, and meditation is an art that teaches the use of eyes, lungs, abdomen, spine, and all the rest. Moreover the place of meditation is important, whether it be the neat, dimly-lighted room or the wide open spaces. And then, of course, meditation is good for mental and bodily health. In the temple you may be told that Zen will inure you against cold and flu, and that by constant practice you have a better chance of surviving the threat of air pollution.

I once attended a convention on meditation at a Zen temple near Kyoto. Experts spoke about yoga, about esoteric Buddhism, and about Zen. We all sat silently in the big meditation hall, and we also did yoga exercises—to the best of our ability. These latter were a preparation for entrance into *samadhi*, and I really believe they can be just that. We heard talks about the technique of meditation—how to stretch and relax, how to sit, and so on; and one of the speakers had a large chart of the human body with which he explained the *chakras* (those centers of psychic energy that yoga speaks of), the course of the "breath" through the body, and all the rest. At the end of each meditation we chanted in unison, "Om, shantih, shantih, shantih!"

The surprising thing about the meeting was the lack of any common faith. No one seemed the slightest bit interested in what anyone else believed or disbelieved, and no one, as far as I recall, even mentioned the name of God. It was just meditation, and only the physical aspects were touched upon. These, however, were discussed in great detail, down to the impact of meditation on the sexual life.

I was the only Christian speaker and, quite frankly, I was a bit nonplussed. I felt that whatever I might say would be irrelevant. I couldn't tell anyone how to stand on his head or stretch his biceps, and it was difficult to speak about God at that meeting. But can one speak about Christian meditation without reference to God? I finally took a cue from one of the speakers who had insisted that meditation, far from stopping with the body, must radiate out to the world of the spirit and to the cosmic dimensions of reality. This, I felt, was the best approach to God in such a gathering.

All in all I learned a lot at that meeting. It was a pleasant and profitable weekend, marred only by the fact that one fellow snored and groaned all night in our communal room so that I didn't get a wink of sleep. The others didn't seem to mind too much. No doubt they were better yogis than I. Or perhaps they had better nerves.

Christians should think more about the role of the body in prayer. After all, there is a lot to be said for beginning meditation where you are. This is particularly true for modern people. Many will call in question the existence of God and the existence of life after death, but only the extremists will call in question the existence of their own body. So why not begin with something they believe in, and through the body go out to the cosmos and to God? In this way, meditation can be taught to people who have little faith—to those who are troubled in conscience or fear that God is dead. Such people can always sit and breathe. For them meditation becomes a search, and I have found, from my little experience in our own place in Tokyo, that people who begin to search in this way eventually find God. Not the anthropomorphic God they have rejected, but the great being in whom we live, move, and are. But the body comes first; God comes at the end.

For the fact is that Western prayer is not sufficiently visceral— it is preoccupied with the brain and not with the deeper layers of the body where the power to approach the spiritual is generated. But we can now study the physical aspects of meditation even scientifically, thanks to experiments at such places as the Buddhist Komazawa University in Tokyo. Here are instruments for testing the physical condition of the person engaged in Zen. Students measure the breathing, the heartbeat, the eye movement, the metabolism, the balance, the brain waves, and just about everything. Similar experiments are being conducted in the United States, and eventually these studies may come up with some suggestions about the ideal conditions for meditation in regard to diet, bodily posture, surroundings, and so on. Needless to say, all this study becomes a bit ridiculous when you find people wandering around with little gadgets to measure alpha waves. But absurdities exist everywhere and cannot be avoided. Moreover, this scientific study need not lead to crass materialism. While visiting Komazawa University once, I asked the professor in charge if he could judge the depth of people's Zen. "No, we cannot measure Zen," he answered, "because the mind is a mystery. All we can measure is the physical repercussions." I was interested to hear him make such a distinction.

Here I might add in parenthesis that Zen does not go in for the minute control of the body that has made yoga famous. In general, Zen flatly rejects anything that smacks of magic or the extraordinary. There may, however, be some exceptions to this. Once I came across a temple far out in the countryside where it was said that the *roshi* performed miraculous feats such as plunging a sharp sword into his stomach without sustaining injury, or taking on himself the sickness of other people so that they were cured. Furthermore, a person whose word I trust told me that he had seen this sharp sword feat with his own eyes and did not doubt its authenticity. But this particular *roshi* is considered quite unorthodox. Discontented with Japanese Zen, he went to China and India as a young man, and on his return started his own form of *zazen*, which he claimed was a direct importation from China. Other branches of Zen, as I have said, despise such extraordinary phenomena and regard them as dangerous distractions on the way to the imageless experience which is *satori*. Strange phenomena go by the generic name of *makyo*, which literally means "the world of the devil" but is applied to all forms of illusion in Zen. In this respect, Japanese Zen is very healthy and liberates itself from abuses found in other forms of mysticism. The *makyo* doctrine of rejecting strange phenomena is remarkably like that of John of the Cross. Again, it is the "nothing, nothing, nothing." One must not be distracted from the goal by spiritual or bodily phenomena of any kind.

Turning now to Christianity, we find that tradition in the West says more about the body than is generally recognized today. It used to be axiomatic (and in my opinion still is) that if you want to lead a life of meditation you must control your eyes, your ears,

your tongue, your hands, and your very gait. All this used to
go by the general name of modesty, a virtue about which we
don't hear much today. It is much stressed in Zen, though the
way of describing it is different. In addition to this, however,
Christian tradition says that meditation transforms the body and
makes it beautiful. The author of *The Cloud* speaks in enthusias-
tically glowing terms of the beautiful physical repercussions of
contemplative prayer. Even the most ugly person, he says, will
become fair and attractive to everyone: his face will be suffused
with joy and a certain grace and peace will accompany his every
action. This is because the inner glory that comes from prayer
cannot but break through and penetrate the body.

One is reminded of Moses descending from the mountain. So
bright and glorious was the joy that suffused his countenance that
the Israelites could not look at him and begged him to wear a
veil—for the very glory of God radiated from the countenance
of the great Israelite. I like to interpret the transfiguration of
Christ as a repetition of this—Christ who is the second Moses,
the reality of which Moses is the type. Quite suddenly, in the
presence of those three astonished men, the inner beauty of Jesus
broke forth over his whole personality, so that his face shone
with an unearthly beauty and his clothes (yes, the inner beauty
extended to his very garments) became dazzling white, with a
whiteness no bleacher on earth could equal. In short, his body
shared in the inexpressible inner beauty.

Probably most of us at some time or other have met people
who share in the bodily beauty of the transfigured Christ. By
television standards they may be pretty ugly—no advertiser in his
right mind would dream of using their faces to sell toothpaste or
soap—but the glory of prayer penetrates their body as it penetrated the body of Moses. I suppose, too, that this is the kind of

beauty that monks and nuns should aim at, now that the changing culture makes them change their exterior way of life and dress. It might be a good idea if, instead of looking to London and Paris, they looked to Moses and Exodus for an ideal of beauty that would help modern man in his search for truth.

Be that as it may, while Christian tradition has affirmed the beauty imparted to the body through meditation, it has been slower in using the body as a way to *samadhi*. Here again, then, we can learn from the East; and to illustrate the role of the body I would like to quote from the *Bhagavad Gita*. This classic work is not, of course, Zen nor even Buddhist, though it seems to have considerable Buddhist influence. But it appeals greatly to me. I am further encouraged to use it here after reading a recent book of Professor R. C. Zaehner, who insists that anyone trying to bridge the gap between Zen and Christianity cannot afford to neglect the *Gita*. This, he claims, is one of the great links between East and West.

In the Sixth Part of the *Gita*, the yogi is told to integrate himself, standing apart, alone and in complete renunciation—"devoid of earthly hope, nothing possessing." Then comes a description of meditation.

> Let him for himself set up
> A steady seat in a clean place
> Neither too high nor yet too low
> With cloth or hides or grass bestrewn
>
> There let him sit and make his mind a single point
> Let him restrain the motions of his thought and senses
> And engage in spiritual exercise
> To purify the self
>
> Remaining still, let him keep body, head and neck
> In a straight line unmoving

Let him fix his gaze on the tip of his nose
Not looking round about him

There let him sit, his self all stilled
His fear all gone, firm in his vow of chastity
His mind controlled, his thoughts on Me
Integrated yet intent on Me*

Glancing at the above, I would like to refer briefly to three points. First of all, the stress on place. This should be neat and clean, not too high nor yet too low. In Zen, too, the place is of the greatest importance. How wonderfully Dogen chose the site of his monastery Eiheiji, still far out in the countryside and plunged in deep silence. The Zen temple attaches great importance to proximity to nature, to the sound of the river or the waterfall, to the Japanese garden and all the rest. Meditation, after all, is not performed by a pure spirit but by a man with a human body.

Now even though there is unending talk today about ecology and environment, the Christian West has made a poor showing in the ecology of religious things. I mean that our Christian churches, especially those recently built, are poor places indeed for meditation. The old Catholic churches had more to be said for them because they at least had a center—a tabernacle before which hung a red lamp—and this provided a focus for the eyes. And there was atmosphere and warmth. Anyone who knows anything about meditation recognizes that you need a place to focus the eyes; if your eyes begin to wander you are lost. The old tabernacle served this purpose, and nothing has taken its place. I believe that many of the old unlettered people who knelt before the tabernacle for hours in places like the Carmelite Church in

*From the book *Hindu Scriptures*, R. C. Zaehner, trans. Everyman's Library Edition (New York: E. P. Dutton & Co., 1966), p. 275. Reprinted by permission of the publisher.

Grafton Street in Dublin fell quickly into *samadhi*. These people were mystics, as enlightened as any *roshi*, and there have been thousands of such people throughout the world. But I ask myself if they will be able to meditate as well in the churches we have now provided for them. I ask myself if the people who built these new churches thought about meditation at all or had any experience of it. And the same holds true for monasteries and convents. I wonder how much thought is now given to the ecology of the thing—to the relationship between buildings and prayer, between clothing and prayer, between corridors and chapels and prayer.

The second point I would like to note in my quotation from the *Gita* is the magnificent posture. The back is straight, the eyes are fixed on the tip of the nose or between the eyebrows; there is no looking around. Later in the *Gita* the stillness of the mind is compared to that of a flame in a windless place. This is a fine simile, because this meditation has all the power and yet all the stillnesss of the flame that rises up in a place where there is no breeze. And all this leads to joy and to a great absence of fear. It is supported by the vow of chastity, the vow of the *bramachari*, who is celibate and chaste.

Here I would like to observe, however, that all Christian prayer need not (and indeed should not) be limited to the lotus posture. There are other positions, such as standing, kneeling, prostration, sitting, and even walking, and often these are determined by the character of the person or the culture to which he belongs. But the posture, whichever it is, is of the greatest importance. Vaguely slouching in a comfortable chair does not lead to depth in meditation.

The third point the one that makes Zaehner insist that the *Gita* can be a bridge between East and West, is the theocentric character of the passage I have quoted. The gaze is fixed on "Me"; that is, on God. The personality is unified in itself in order that all the faculties may be fixed on God, who is present in the deepest part of the soul—or, more correctly, who *is* the deepest part of the soul, since in man there is a divine spark. In this the *Gita* comes much nearer to Christianity than does Zen.

The yogi seated in magnificent meditation has all the bodily beauty of which the author of *The Cloud* speaks. This beauty is common to contemplatives of every religious tradition, and it is a beauty that the modern world unconsciously seeks.

CHAPTER 9

BREATHING AND RHYTHM

It stands to reason that in any kind of meditation control of the mind is of primary importance. Most of us have some idea about control of our body—our arms and legs and the rest—but control of the mind is a more difficult business. And it is in this that the East excels. That this control is no small task, however, is stressed in the *Gita*. "Fickle is the mind," says Arjuna, "impetuous, exceeding strong. How difficult to curb it! As easy curb the wind, I say." To which the Blessed Lord answers, "Herein there is no doubt. Hard is the mind to curb and fickle; but by untiring effort and by transcending passion it can be held in check."* In short, the mind is hard to curb, but the task is not impossible. Control is possible. But how?

One of the oldest ways of controlling the mind is through breathing. Everyone knows from experience how intimate is the connection between breath and the psychic life. When we are excited or jealous or angry, the breath comes short and fast. On the other hand, when we are calm and collected, or deep in concentration or meditation, the breath slows down and even seems to stop. One recalls the beautiful line of Wordsworth: "The holy time is quiet as a nun, breathless with adoration." In the depths of adoration one may become so silent that one is breathless. This happens also in Zen: the breath slows and almost stops, so that one simply hears the beating of the heart.

* *Hindu Scriptures*, op. cit., p. 277.

77

If the psychic condition affects the breathing, it is equally true that consciousness of the breath can help control the psychic life. If one is emotionally upset, regular breathing may help to soothe the nerves and calm the mind.

As for meditation, it is recommended in Zen to begin with a deep breath (if the back is straight this will be abdominal) which is held for a moment and then exhaled. I know a Zen master who encourages his disciples to take this deep breath whenever they change their occupation or begin some new kind of work. The breath helps one leave the old and start the new with total concentration.

One way of beginning Zen is by counting the breathing. I myself did not begin this way (I had a different initiation, as I have already said), so I feel a little diffident about describing it. But anyhow, here is how it is taught. One begins by counting each inhalation and exhalation, one on the intake and two on the output of breath, counting to ten. While counting, one concentrates just on the breath. When this has been done for some time (a few days perhaps) one can count simply on the exhalation without counting on the inhalation at all. Again, when this has been done for some time, one counts only on the inhalation. Finally, one stops counting altogether and simply "follows the breath" or is conscious of the fact that one is breathing.

Now this may sound like a gimmick—some Christians react against this kind of thing and scoff at the idea of calling it meditation at all. But it should be remembered that, apart from calming the emotions, this concentration has the effect of banishing the reasoning and thinking and imagining that go on at the superficial level of psychic life, and thus paves the way for a deeper unification. It, so to speak, silences the upper, superficial layers of the mind so that it becomes possible to concentrate at a deeper level and with a consciousness that is ordinarily dormant.

Thoughts and images are brushed aside; one is conscious only of the breathing, and then the deeper sectors of unconscious life surge up into consciousness.

In the *Soto* sect (which uses the *koan* much less than *Rinzai*) concentration on the breath—without counting—is stressed very much even for those who are well advanced. Without it, there is always the danger that one may lose all recollection and unification and simply waste one's time. For Christians, the very sitting and breathing, performed in silent faith, can itself be an act of adoration. Western people, as I have pointed out many times, think that they are not meditating unless they are using their brain. But can there not be a form of meditation in which one sits and breathes and lets the heart beat? Surely total silence can be a wonderful expression of adoration.

Besides, breath rises from the very root of the being, so that consciousness of the breath can lead to a realization of the deepest self by opening up new doors in the psychic life. In the Bible it is clear that breath is identified with the deepest thing in man; it is precisely when breath enters into matter that man becomes man.

Further, it should be remembered that in Eastern thought breath is not only the little breath in my little body. It is much more than this. It is associated with the breath of the cosmos, so that regulating the breath means regulating one's relationship with the whole cosmos and bringing about harmony and order. This is true of both Zen and Yoga, where breath plays such an important part. In the Judaeo-Christian tradition, the breath is associated with the Holy Spirit, who is *spiratio* and fills the universe. Hence the symbolism of Jesus "breathing" on his apostles—"Receive ye the Holy Spirit. . . ." Hence also the wind that shakes the building prior to the descent of the Spirit on the apostles. Reflecting on all this, one can see how consciousness of the breath can be truly Christian prayer because it can be consciousness of the Spirit in total forgetfulness of self. I believe that a whole method of Christian prayer associated with the breathing could be developed. But perhaps the time for this has not yet arrived.

Not that consciousness of the breathing is foreign to the Christian tradition. Here are some of the directions to the Hesychasts that we find in the *Philokalia*.

You know, brother, how we breathe; we breathe the air in and out. On this is based the life of the body and on this depends its warmth. So, sitting down in your cell, collect your mind, lead it into the path of the breath along which the air enters in, constrain it to enter the heart altogether with the inhaled air, and keep it there. Keep it there, but do not leave it silent and idle; instead give it the following prayer: "Lord, Jesus Christ, Son of God, have mercy upon me." Let this be its constant occupation, never to be abandoned. For this work, by keeping the mind free from dreaming, renders it unassailable to suggestions of the enemy and leads it to Divine desire and love. Moreover, brother, strive to accustom your mind not to come out too soon; for at first it feels very lonely in that inner seclusion and imprisonment. But when it gets accustomed to it, it begins on the contrary to dislike darting about among external things. For the kingdom of God is within us, and for a man who has seen it within, and having found it through pure prayer, has experienced it, everything outside loses its attraction and value. It is no longer unpleasant and wearisome for him to be within.*

In the tradition to which the above quotation belongs there is not, as far as I know, any counting, but only the repetition of an ejaculation in unison with the breath. This ejaculation can take the

* Writings from the *"Philokalia on Prayer of the Heart,"* E. Kadloubovsky and G. E. H. Palmer, trans. (London: Faber & Faber, 1951).

form given above or it can simply be the repetition of the word "Jesus." Some writers say that with the inhalation Jesus comes in, and with the exhalation "I" go out, and in this way the personality is filled with Christ. As can be seen from the words I have quoted, the ejaculation purifies the mind of all thoughts and desires and distractions so that it enters deep down into the psychic life in total nudity of spirit.

The practice of repeating an ejaculation is found especially in the Amida sect of Buddhism where the words *Namu Amida Butsu* (Honor to the Buddha Amida) are repeated again and again and again. Zen does not speak much about this so-called *nembutsu*, but I was surprised once while visiting a Zen temple to hear one of the young monks say that he made use of the *nembutsu*. He said that at first it was himself repeating the words *"Namu Amida Butsu,"* but in time it was no longer "I" repeating the words, but just *"Namu Amida Butsu"* without any subject at all—for the "I" was gone. For him the *nembutsu* was a way to the nonself condition that is so characteristic of Zen. I was interested in this and recalled the thesis of Dr. Suzuki that silent nothingness and the *koan* and the *nembutsu* all lead to the same goal; namely, enlightenment. In all cases, the upper levels of psychic life are purified and cleansed, thus allowing the deep levels of unconscious life to surge into consciousness and give enlightenment.

Be that as it may, the repetition of an ejaculation can enter so deeply into the psychic life that it becomes almost automatic and continues even in the busiest moments. Some Buddhists claim that the rhythm of the *nembutsu* goes on even in time of sleep. A Japanese nun told me of how she once sat by the bedside of a dying sister. This latter had had an operation and was barely conscious; yet she kept repeating the words "Jesusu awaremi tamae" (Jesus have mercy on me) in a way that seemed quite effortless and almost automatic. This kind of thing is not, in my opinion, very unusual.

I myself believe that the repetition of an ejaculation or the consciousness of the breathing is somehow linked to a basic rhythm in the body, a rhythm that can be deepened and deepened until it reaches the center of one's being from which enlightenment breaks forth. Let me try to explain what I mean.

There is a basic rhythm in the body, linked to a consciousness that is deeper than is ordinarily experienced. When man was in his natural setting, working in the fields or fishing in the sea, this rhythm was probably easy enough to find, because man's rapport with his surroundings was harmonious. And in such a setting man was more open to cosmic forces, less inclined to atheism. Recall that the apostles were fishermen, and that Christianity is closely bound up with fishing. But with the advent of urbanization this rhythm and harmony were lost; man became out of tune with his surroundings. That is where we now stand. Again it is a problem of ecology. We have to cope not only with air pollution but also with a rival rhythm that comes from the Beatles, the Rolling Stones, and a number of forces that jolt our psychic life. Excessive noise, it is well known, dulls not only the sense of hearing but also the sense of smell and of sight. How much more, then, does it dull the deeper layers of psychic life! Small wonder if it deadens the profounder rhythm that should be within us.

But anyone who wants to meditate in depth must find this rhythm and the consciousness that accompanies it. And people find their rhythm in various ways. For some it is through the breathing, and this alone is sufficient. For others it is the breathing linked to an ejaculation. Or again it may be the repetition of an ejaculation without any thought of breathing whatever. Or again,

some people find their rhythm by consciousness of the beating
of the heart, and not infrequently an ejaculation is attached to
this rather than to the breath. I have known people, too, who
discover this rhythm simply by walking. A friend of mine goes
for a walk every morning before breakfast, repeating an ejaculation. As he walks, the ejaculation becomes automatic (it fits in
with the rhythm) and just goes on, to such an extent that he
becomes oblivious to his surroundings. He has not yet told me
how he copes with the danger of traffic accidents, and I have not
asked him. But this is what I mean by saying that an ejaculation
fits in with the basic rhythm.

Perhaps all this has something in common with listening to
music. Most people have had the experience of being haunted
for several days by a beautiful melody they have heard. The
music continues within and simply will not go away. In some such
way, the Jesus prayer or the *nembutsu* continues in the psychic
life of those who are in love with the object to which these
ejaculations point. There is, however, one significant difference.
Sometimes the haunting music may disturb us. We want to put it
away and we can't; it is persistent, even at times tyrannical. Now
the rhythmic ejaculation is never like that. Probably this is because it is much, much deeper. The music, I believe, does not
enter the deepest layer of psychic life; it remains somehow
external to us, and that is why it can jar and even cause discord—
because it can be at odds with that other rhythm which is deeper.
The ejaculation, on the other hand, wells up from the deepest
point of our being and is not external at all. It is the expression
of the deepest self.

Formerly many people seem to have found this rhythm through
the rosary. Take the case of those old women living near the sea—
women who saw their sons mauled and murdered by the cruel
Atlantic waves—whose lives were spent in the repetition of the

rosary until their fingers were callous with the feel of the beads. These people found their rhythm through the rosary and through suffering. They were deeply enlightened.

For those of us who live in the city, the problem is acute. Life in the countryside in proximity to nature is undoubtedly a great advantage for one who wants to meditate, as the great contemplative orders discovered long ago. Yet I believe that the great noisy cities like Tokyo (which I love) are not an insuperable obstacle. Once the rhythm is found it transcends environment, and place ceases to matter. The ecology problem can be solved at this level too.

As I have said, the rhythm of breath or ejaculation leads to something deeper. All points to the center of the soul, the core of the being, the sovereign point of the spirit, the divine spark, the true self, the realm from which enlightenment arises. This is the truest thing that exists.

CHAPTER 10

PROGRESS

All kinds of people practice Zen or contemplation or *samadhi* at a superficial level, but those who go deep are few. On this point most spiritual traditions agree. The *Gita* states that one in a thousand devotes himself to meditation, and of those who do, one in a thousand goes the whole way. John of the Cross writes his books like a man in a hurry, as if to say, "I don't want to write about the early stages of this ascent because there are plenty of books written about it already. I want to talk about the later stages, almost unknown because seldom experienced." As for the *roshi*, they speak of the kindergarten level to which many arrive, while few carry on to the level of university graduation. In short, many are called but few are chosen. Thousands jostle at the narrow gate but few get through. If you go in search of a just man, you don't find him easily.

It has always struck me as sad that this should be so. After all, the world needs great mystics, not just the small fry, and how wonderful it would be to find a formula for leading people the whole way. Or what on earth stops people from going the whole hog? Why do they stick at the kindergarten or even the high-school stage without going on to graduation?

Yet in my sober moments I know that this is a question that shouldn't be asked and cannot be answered. For progress in mysticism is linked with vocation. Most people remain small fry because they are meant to remain small fry. Mother Nature is not prodigal with genius. She seldom gives birth to saints, and when she does, she squirms and wriggles and yells in the writhing agony of parturition. Or she shakes the pillars of the temple till it falls down and crushes everybody. Occasionally, of course, one meets the saint; and then one meets someone who has suffered in the depth of his being and has tasted the anguish of Gethsemane. Such persons are rare. Usually they are not the people who write books and wander around the world on lecture tours. These latter are often children playing in the sand and looking wistfully toward the rich and teeming bed of the ocean. They are not called to explore it except from afar.

Yet when all is said, it still remains sad that saints are so rare. And it is not impossible that we could have one or two more, if the human obstacles that cross their path were removed. This problem preoccupied me for some time, and I once proposed it for discussion to a group of Buddhists and Christians which had gathered informally to talk about meditation. All agreed that the problem was a valid one, so we talked about removing obstacles and helping people ascend the mountain.

One of the Buddhists remarked that the greatest obstacle is fear. This impressed me quite a lot, and I felt instinctively that it was terribly true. He said that Buddhist art is full of wild beasts that symbolize the terrors of the great descent into the center of one's being. And he further added, from his own experience, that there comes a time when one simply does not want to sit down on that little cushion to do *zazen*. The very thought of it makes one tremble. Or one wants to run out of the meditation hall (Westerners in Japan sometimes disgrace themselves by doing just this, but Japanese are more long-suffering) and get away. Just to get away. In such circumstances, he went on to say, one is greatly helped by the community or by the system. The order of time obliges one to go to the meditation hall—there is no way out—and it carries one through.

All this threw light on John of the Cross for me. I recalled his words in the *Spiritual Canticle*:

> I will pluck no flowers; I will fear no wild beasts.

To pluck no flowers is to practice the most radical detachment in the face of the seductive beauty of a world that might hinder one's pursuit of the very source of beauty and of love. The fearful wild beasts are those of Buddhist art; they represent the terrors of the mystical descent. Perhaps biblical authors, too, realize how cramping is fear, because all through the Bible like a great refrain echo the words,

> Fear not. I am.

One most somehow conquer one's fear, one must lose one's fear. Perhaps the best way is to smile blithely at the yawning jaws of those romping wild beasts—to look down their gaping throats and laugh. Because in fact they cannot hurt at all. You don't have to kill them or fight with them; it is enough to laugh at them. This is detachment. If you fear them, they smell your fear (just like your neighbor's dog), and then you get bitten. My Buddhist friend was carried beyond fear by pressure from the system; but the Westerner in the seventies is less likely to be saved in this way, since "system" is a naughty word linked to an establishment that cramps or persecutes. Yet whatever way it is done, the seductive flowers and the roaring beasts must not be allowed to stand in the way of progress.

One might ask, of course, what in God's name there is to fear and what these beasts are anyway.

First of all I would say that there is fear of the effort involved. Mysticism is no soft affair. You don't go into the desert to see a reed shaken by the wind or a man clothed in soft garments. Everybody shrinks from the inexorable law of renunciation. Think of what is involved in the shattering Buddhist vow recited daily in the temple:

> However inexhaustible our passions,
> We vow to uproot them all.

In Christianity the message is often expressed in terms of death and life. Unless the grain of wheat falling to the ground dies, itself alone remains. One must lose one's life. There is no escape from death. And this death is no breezy metaphor. One must lose the very grasp upon one's ego (and what a terrible thing this is), only to find a new ego—and it is then that the joy of enlightenment fills the personality.

There is yet another reason for fear. In the mystic journey you go alone into the darkness. Modern man is well aware of the ghosts and goblins and murky secrets that lurk in the subliminal sectors of his mind. Good reason to fear them. At the bottom, of course, joy and beauty await us, but other things are released on the way down. I myself believe that within us are locked up torrents and torrents of joy that can be released by meditation—sometimes they will burst through with incredible force, flooding the personality with an extraordinary happiness that comes from one knows not where. This is true of contemplation; it is true of Zen; it is true of yoga (how it is stressed in the *Gita!*); it is found in the *Acts of the Apostles* and mirrored in the Pentecostal movement. One can be suffused with a joy that makes celibacy intelligible and worth while. But, and this is the point here, mystics who have penetrated deeply into reality have discovered evil also, evil that has shaken them to the roots of their being, so that they have sweated blood like one who fell on his face in Gethsemane. For deep, deep down at the center of things is darkness as well as light, death as well as life, hell as well as heaven. The dragons, the beasts, and the whore of the *Apocalypse* speak of something real. If even the LSD trip can have its destructive hell, if it can be a traumatic and hair-raising experience, the same may be said of the mystical descent. The wars and the hatred, the concentration camps and the tortures, the sex crimes and the murders, lurk in the unconscious realms of the mind and in the depth of reality. It would be unrealistic to think of mysticism in terms of unalloyed joy. Evil, alas, is a fact of existence, and I have met people whose mystical experience has been accompanied by horrendous fear.

Again, for Christians there may be another fearful experience, expressed by the kind old *roshi* who said that God would disappear and only Johnston San would remain. It has happened to Christian mystics that, at times, God has disappeared and they have felt totally abandoned in awful loneliness, clinging only to a faith that is like night. To say this, of course, is not to deny God but simply to say that he cannot be known directly by the natural human powers, and the time may come when he is no longer experienced as present. Perhaps this is because, when experience becomes intense (as in great mental suffering), it seems like no experience at all, because one is completely numbed. And this, too, seems to have happened to the mystics. Small wonder if those who go deep come up against a crisis or even a breakdown, or become temporary misfits in society. At this moment they may need the help of a director. And this brings me to another point that is crucial for meditation.

Zen is dominated by the towering figure of the *roshi*. When the stars fall and the moon is turned to blood and the mountains tremble, he stands serene and unruffled. He is the granite rock rising up out of the swirling and turbulent waters; the disciple pins his faith on him during the critical period of transition between two lives—between the loss of the old and the finding of the new self. He is not unlike the proverbial psychoanalyst to whom the patient clings for desperate support. In this whole matter, Zen is rather like Catholicism—or it might be more modest to say that Catholicism is rather like Zen.

I mean that Catholic tradition has always stressed exterior authority and direction and the rest. It is true, of course, that Catholic authority became too juridical. So many Catholics are shouting about this today that I need not add my raucous voice to the happy choir. But the clear-cut principle of the director and the directed stands out pretty ruggedly. And then there are Thomas and Albert, Bonaventure and somebody else, Ignatius and his companions, and lots of others. Catholicism, I feel obliged to state, has stressed direction partly from the long-established conviction, born from the accumulated wisdom of centuries, that every potential mystic needs an occasional kick in the pants lest he—or she—fall into conceit, attachments, and all the tomfoolery popularly known as bloody nonsense. Consequently, the face-slapping, the back-walloping, the nose-tweaking, and the rest are neither out of place nor irrelevant. Yet the role of the Master is not just this; nor is it simply to give information—which in any case you can get from a book—but to steer people through to enlightenment and even to clobber them with a salutary shock that will kill and resurrect.

I believe it is not just fanciful to see this technique put into practice by Christ, the great guru who knocked people into enlightenment with remarkable power. Take the case of the Gentile woman who asked for help. "It is wrong to take the bread of the children and throw it to the dogs," warns Jesus, issuing a slap in the face that parallels anything in Zen. But the woman comes through. She takes it squarely. She dies. "Even the little dogs," she cries, "eat the crumbs that fall from the table of the children." And with this total loss she receives the enlightenment for which she craves. "Go home. The unclean spirit has left your daughter."

The pattern of death and resurrection stands out boldly here, just as it does in the other passages where Jesus asks for total death. Sell what you have and give to the poor. If you do that you'll get enlightenment. But if you prefer to be like the camel trying to get through the eye of the needle. . . . Perhaps every religious tradition teaches that you only get enlightenment through the complete loss that is death. Think of Abraham. For him Isaac was everything, and it was only when he was ready to kill his son, his only son, that he heard the tremendous promise that the nations of the earth would be blessed in his offspring. Here again is his enlightenment. And what I say here is true, the main task of the Master is to help you die in order that you may live.

Today, however, we hear the sad complaint that competent gurus just can't be found, and this complaint is voiced not only in the West but also in Japan and India. Alas, the theological market is flooded with Ph.D.'s (or is it S.T.D.'s?) sauntering around looking for jobs, but if you want a decent guru where do you find him? This lack sometimes prompts people to look outside their own religious tradition, a Christian to a Buddhist *roshi* or vice versa. But I honestly don't buy this idea, and I doubt if it works. While the death and resurrection motif is similar and a Buddhist can clobber you as effectively as a Christian, the fact remains that the underlying faith is different: it is one thing to

believe in Christ and another thing to believe in the Buddha nature. And this has to be faced honestly. It doesn't help to get
things mixed up.

It seems to me that Christians must put some effort into forming their own directors or *roshi*. This means fewer Ph.D.'s and
more gurus; less study and more meditation; fewer universities
and more meditation halls. Ordinarily speaking, enlightenment is
passed on from Master to disciple and on and on, but when a
link is missing in the chain relationship, some people must be
driven by the Spirit into the desert to fast and pray and hear the
voice of God. And others, then, must stop badgering them about
getting into classrooms and teaching mathematics.

On the other hand I have sometimes asked myself, and others
also, if it is possible to dispense with the *roshi* altogether and do
your dying and resurrecting in another way. I was made to think
of this while attending a quiet little *sesshin* in Kyoto, where professors and students practiced Zen for seven days without a *roshi*.
Instead of *dokusan* they opened their interior life to one another.
At a fixed time, when all were sitting in *zazen*, one could choose
any of the participants as one's director. He would simply kneel
in front of the person of his choice and make a profound bow;
then both of them would toddle off to a quiet room where a short
chat was possible. Whether or not this method is completely
successful I don't know. I merely mention it as a possibility.

There is yet another possibility, and I will refer to it again in
my next and final chapter. It is not impossible that in Christianity the role of the guru or roshi can be played not by one man
but by the community. This came home to me when I saw the
Pentecostal movement in the United States. It is not impossible
that the imposition of hands, the outward shock, and the charismatic prayer may have an effect rather like the clobbering of the
roshi. If this is so, it would mean that a Christian Zen needs

something like the charismatic renewal for its completion; and similarly, the charismatic renewal may well benefit from the silence of *zazen*. But more about this below.

There are two final points I would like to mention when speaking of progress. The first is that progress in Zen or contemplation is, I believe, linked to age. I mean that, just as Aristotle held that young and emotional people were not good subjects for philosophy, something similar may possibly be said of the higher reaches of contemplative life. It is true, of course, that young people (if they are tough) have some advantages in the grueling practice of Japanese Zen, but when it comes to the still and silent depths, a certain age is probably an advantage. Jung says somewhere that the middle period of life—thirty-five to forty-five—often sees the beginning of contemplation. Indeed, if I read him correctly, he says that people ought to become contemplative in these years if their psychic life goes well. These years, the psychologists tell us, are often accompanied by violent eruptions and desperation and sexual upheaval. But they are also the years of opportunity, the time of contemplative awakening. Perhaps the traditional Oriental esteem for age is based on the realization that there is a certain level of contemplative wisdom inaccessible to youth and enjoyed by the old if their psychic development has gone well.

And the last point. I believe that celibacy is of great help for anyone who wants to get deep in a thing like Zen. So much has been said and written about celibacy recently that I hesitate to toss off a few half-baked ideas. Nevertheless I hope I will be forgiven for stating my views in all simplicity.

After all, what is the value of celibacy? We have heard that the celibate is more available, or more "open," or that he has more time. Or it is suggested that whoever wants to devote himself to the severe discipline of meditation just cannot afford to have a woman breathing down his neck night and day. Or it is said that the married man is all tied up with his wife and kids. All this may well be true. But the ancient Oriental reverence for celibacy does not stem from this. It derives from the belief that the celibate person (if he is truly chaste) has increased spiritual power. Probably this is because his sexual energy is converted into spiritual energy. This gives the celibate a distinct advantage in the pursuit of wisdom and in the practice of contemplative love. It makes him a better candidate for mysticism. Besides, detachment is of the very essence of mysticism, and I doubt if there is any detachment that cuts so deeply into the human fiber as celibacy. It creates an awful loneliness at the core of one's being—and it is precisely from this emptiness that the blind stirring of love takes it origin. This loneliness opens the doors of perception to an inner world that might otherwise be inaccessible. It creates the best soil for mysticism.

If celibacy is little esteemed in modern Christianity, this may be due to a lack of mysticism. The two somehow go hand in hand. Not that all mystics must be celibate—they may well be married —but the celibate has advantages, and a culture that esteems mysticism will not despise celibacy. Perhaps the so-called crisis of celibacy in the Catholic Church is also a crisis of mysticism.

CHAPTER 11

ENLIGHTENMENT

One cannot write about Zen without writing about enlightenment. This is the center of the whole thing, as it is indeed the
center of all Buddhism. In enlightenment is found great wisdom
as well as release from the shackles of suffering; and the enlightenment of the Lord Buddha, from which the rest stems, is one of
the great events of history. Though the whole of Zen is geared
to enlightenment, one is faced with the interesting paradox that
one must never desire it. To do so would be to cultivate an attachment that would vitiate the whole process. It is the old story
again: one must desire nothing—and nothing means nothing.

In some Zen sectors in modern Japan, however, there is a
certain amount of gossip about enlightenment. "He (or she) did,
or did not, get enlightenment." A friend of mine, an assiduous
practitioner of Zen, told me that after the *sesshin* in a certain
temple the people were more or less divided into those who got
satori and the also-rans who did not make the grade. This irked
my friend not a little, since he was always amongst the also-rans.
It was not, he protested, just a question of his bruised feelings—
this he could support with philosophy—but righteous indignation
about gossip that stemmed mainly from women who had made
inroads into a discipline that was traditionally masculine and
virile. True Zen, he said, was reticent about the whole business
("he that knows does not speak, and he that speaks does not
know") since it was sacred and intimate, and all this talk was

a deviation from the pristine and genuine spirit. Most true Zen people would, I believe, support his basic thesis. On the other hand *satori*, being a great interior experience, can tempt the poetic temperament to indulge in melodrama about its soul-stirring repercussions. Even Dr. Suzuki cannot be totally exonerated from such touches of melodrama when he writes about enlightenment.

Again it should be remembered that there are various degrees of enlightenment and that some Masters are quicker to recognize and ratify *satori* than others. One hears of stalwarts who have spent decades in assiduous sitting without getting a shred of enlightenment. But this does not mean that they have been wasting their time. Dogen, founder of the Soto sect, insisted that the very sitting is a form of enlightenment, and this again fits in with John of the Cross, who declares that the darkness of contemplation is in itself an enlightenment (for him imageless darkness is faith and faith is enlightenment) even if one never arrives at any soul-stirring experience. And this doctrine is sound. I think it is an error, and no small one, to dramatize the *satori* experience with lurid or beautiful descriptions. It is this that makes Zen look like the kick that comes from drugs. In fact, the important thing is not the sudden shock to one's psychic life but the total transformation that ensues. What matters is the Pauline new man, the new creation that follows the death of the old. I believe that a gradual enlightenment without melodrama should be, and is, possible. The transformation comes slowly but profoundly in people not temperamentally geared to sudden psychic change.

What I want to discuss here, however, is the question of Christian *satori*. If the Christian practices Zen, will he arrive at the same experience as the Buddhist? Or what kind of experience can he be expected to reach? Or is there, in fact, some experience to which constant practice and good direction can lead the well-meaning and determined Christian? I would like to consider three kinds of experience that could be classified as possible Christian versions of *satori*.

First of all I believe that there is a basic enlightenment which is neither Christian nor Buddhist nor anything else. It is just human. Merton was probably referring to this in the letter quoted in Chapter III where he says that in a certain sense one goes beyond all categories, religious or other. This experience it seems to me is found in all cultures, though in modified form, and is an experience of the unity of all things and the loss of self.

T. S. Eliot has written a good deal about this in its relation to aesthetics. I myself have met a Christian monk who told me that before entering the monastery he had a sudden profound *satori*— he didn't know what else to call it—while reading Plato. Later he had other specifically Christian experiences; but this first one struck him as being somehow universal and not specifically Christian, even though it was the thing that prompted him to become a monk. To me this was interesting because I had always believed that Plato was a deeply enlightened man, and that underlying his beautiful Greek is a basic *satori* of great profundity.

The second kind of possible *satori* is specifically Judaeo-Christian. It is the experience of Paul on the road to Damascus, when he fell from his horse in the blinding light and heard the words of Jesus. Or the experience of Moses told to take off his shoes because the ground was holy. Or that of Isaiah and the prophets. Together with this I would classify the transfiguring "wound" of John of the Cross and Teresa and others. Such experiences are deeply interesting, but they are so far removed from the Zen way of speaking that I would hesitate to put them in the same category. They are much more bound up with vocation; they are for few people; no methodology leads to this kind of thing.

The third kind of experience, and the one in which I see the most possibility, is that of conversion or "metanoia." This, I believe, is the central religious experience demanded by the gospel and expressed in the Baptist's words: "Repent, for the kingdom of God is at hand." The words "conversion" or "repentance" have now, unfortunately, very ethical overtones—"she is converted because she no longer drinks whiskey"—but the original meaning was not this. Conversion was a change of mind and heart, and its most vivid expression is found in the Acts of the Apostles and the epistles of Paul, where we read of the baptism of the Spirit that follows the imposition of Christian hands. What a big experience it was! And it is still alive in the world today. Sometimes those who receive it speak in tongues, so deeply are they affected; and it is accompanied by a release of joy not unlike that which floods the personality in *satori*. The most remarkable effect is the proclamation that Jesus is the Lord and the inclination to praise him. I believe that this conversion experience is found, too, in the Fourth Gospel, where it is a seeing— "whereas I was blind, now I see." It is the opening of blind eyes which now come to see the glory of Christ. "We have seen his glory . . . ."

In the centuries that followed the apostolic age, it was customary to lead people to this deeply-felt experience of metanoia, just as the Zen master leads his disciples to *satori*—though the methodology, of course, was quite different. Metanoia was no exceptional thing. It did not differ from ordinary faith; it was just that this faith could be experienced again and again in a series of "conversions." As late as the sixteenth century we find Ignatius of Loyola with a methodology called *The Spiritual Exercises* for leading people precisely to this great and traditional conversion. He unabashedly expected some people to come to an experience resembling that of Paul on the road to Damascus (as I have said,

I myself would not be so ambitious), and he certainly discovered a method for leading people to great depth in the spirit. However, in the period after Trent, the Catholic Church, though it maintained the basic teaching on conversion or metanoia, became suspicious of certain kinds of religious experience, particularly those which seemed to be subjective and emotional, and it was left to some branches of Protestantism to emphasize sudden conversion in its clear-cut Pentecostal dimensions. Now, however, its value is recognized by large numbers of Christians of every denomination, and the so-called charismatic renewal has hit the Church with force.

Now I am not at all suggesting that conversion or metanoia is the same thing as *satori*. What I do say is that the methodology of Zen, if adopted by a Christian, may well culminate in sudden conversion. If Zen is performed in a' Christian atmosphere and surrounded by Christian liturgy, it may bring people to this deep and joyful metanoia. Such an experience, I repeat, has in common with *satori* the fact that it is not far beyond the ordinary psychological powers of man—it is not like the Damascus experience of Paul or the Horeb experience of Moses. It should be the ordinary thing in the Christian life—at all events that is how I understand the New Testament; and without it, faith is still weak and superficial. Let me say, then, briefly how I came to see the value of the sudden metanoia and its relevance for one who practices Zen in a Christian setting.

When I arrived in the United States in the summer of 1970 I heard for the first time about the Catholic Pentecostals. Some people told me they were crackpots who went in for demonstrative prayer (they spoke in tongues, it was said) and generally gave way to a good deal of emotion in their expression of Christian faith. I accepted the crackpot theory rather uncritically since by education, though not by temperament, I steer clear of

emotion in things religious. I suppose I would have been less prejudiced had the term "charismatic renewal" been used. Anyhow,
later in the summer I was staying at a convent on the East Coast
and the nuns suggested that I attend a Catholic Pentecostal group.
Anyone who has had contact with nuns knows that they are
rather persuasive people. So I decided to go to the meeting for
the sake of a quiet life.

A large number of people had gathered in the parish hall:
young and old, black and white, long-haired and short-haired,
bearded and clean-shaven. We sat round in a circle in silence
and then, after some time had passed, people would stand up and
pray spontaneously or read from the Bible or ask for prayers or
share some experience or speak in tongues. The group prayed
together and sang together. I was struck by the combination of
spontaneity and peace and began to lose my prejudice. People
were not acting according to a fixed plan nor according to a set
of rules and regulations—they were following the Spirit. I reflected that people looking for spontaneity often express it in wild
revelry, as in the medieval carnivals and in some modern gim-
micks; or in sensitivity sessions or what not. But here was a
spontaneous expression of deep faith in an atmosphere of peace.
Apart from everything else, it must surely be psychologically
healthy. After the general meeting, we divided into groups in
which some received initial instruction, others asked for prayers
and the imposition of hands, others asked for the baptism of the
Spirit. I myself received the baptism of the Spirit.

All this may seem ten thousand miles from Zen. How could
such a spontaneous, talkative affair have anything to do with the
profound silence of *zazen*? Yet I believe there is a connection.
Because to think that Zen is all silent sitting is an error. It has
another side, an almost irrational side, where people act and shout
with Pentecostal spontaneity and fervor—acting, that is, from

the deepest center of their being and not from the cerebral area of discursive thinking. Zen literature is full of amusing anecdotes about people jumping into ponds or tweaking others' noses or saying strange things. It is true, of course, that they don't speak in tongues; but I have seen them do somewhat similar things. I recall how, at a *sesshin* I attended, after some days some of the participants began to shout out at the top of their voices, "Mu . . . Mu . . . Mu . . . MUuuuuuuuuuuuu!" I took this as a way of getting rid of pent-up energy, for it seemed to burst forth from the very depth of their being, and it reminded me of the Christian mystics who shouted out "Jesus!" or "God!" or whatever it may be at tense moments in their prayer. This kind of phenomenon, it seems to me, indicates that deep psychological forces are at work; it indicates that the person's religious experience has touched a profound level of psychic life. But at the same time it is only a by-product and is not of primary importance. This would seem to be the opinion of Paul, who is always careful to put the gift of tongues in the lower grades of spiritual gifts. The principal thing, he says, is charity.

Returning to the Pentecostal meeting, it seems to me that the imposition of hands, the prayers of the people, the charity of the community—these can be forces that release the psychic power that brings enlightenment to the person who has been consistently practicing *zazen*. In the Christian they bring metanoia. But to come to this you have to die. And when you kneel to receive the baptism of the Spirit, that is what happens. You die. For me personally the baptism of the Spirit was a great event. It gave me some idea of what the early Christians must have experienced. It gave me some inkling of what *satori* must be like.

So I suppose it is true, after all, that the Pentecostals are crackpots, and I would like to be a crackpot too. Because if you want enlightenment you have to become a crackpot; drugs don't do the trick. This is the lesson of both Buddhism and Christianity—it is the doctrine of death and resurrection.

This, then, is what I mean when I say that in the attainment of enlightenment two factors are necessary: the internal meditation and the external happening. Ordinarily speaking, *zazen* or meditation alone is not sufficient, and the exterior imposition of hands alone is not sufficient either. The external pressure of the *roshi* or of the community brings the interior experience to fruition. I heard this put well by an old Master. Coming to enlightenment, he said, you are like the chicken breaking out from the egg. From within the little thing keeps pushing, pushing, pushing, but it never breaks out unless the mother hen pecks on the shell from outside. And in the same way your meditation may keep maturing, maturing, but it will not reach its climax without pressure from outside yourself.

I have mentioned the Pentecostal experience, yet I am not suggesting that it is the only way to conversion or that it is for everyone. I believe that the sacraments may have the same effect: these can be the exterior signs that carry one to the interior breakthrough. If one speaks to enlightened Christians one will find that often they have had their biggest experience at the reception of baptism or of Communion, or again, at the moment of receiving absolution. In this latter case the confessor is firmly in the position of the *roshi*. He is not there as a friendly counselor to give good advice (though he may well do this); he may even act as a judge and force the penitent into conversion like any guru in the East, or like that great guru who walked by the Sea of Galilee. And the penitent dies. He loses everything. Then comes resurrection—the release from mental anguish, the joy, the laughter, the sunshine, the enlightenment. . . .

Anyhow, it was through the Pentecostal movement that I came to see the parallel between the Zen *satori* and the Christian conversion or metanoia. From the time of my first contact with Zen I had been struck by its singlemindedness. I felt (with something approaching envy) that here were people who knew precisely what they wanted in this world whereas Christians were often less sure. This was particularly true as far as Buddhist monks and nuns were concerned. They wanted enlightenment, and there were no two ways about it. As I say, the singleness of purpose impressed me greatly; and only much later did I begin to realize that as Buddhism centers around enlightenment, so Christianity centers around conversion. Change your mind and heart for the kingdom of God is at hand. Change! Turn! This is the perennial call of Christ and the prophets. It is a clarion call, an invitation to rebirth, to a change of consciousness, to becoming a new man.

This, I now see, is what Christianity is all about; for this is faith. Christianity is concerned with an earth–shaking, soul–stirring revolution as stupendous as anything Dr. Suzuki wrote about in his most poetic flights. If we forget this, we end up with a milk–and–water thing that sometimes passes as Christianity but is no more than social respectability.

For me (and, I believe, for many Christians) this basic message could easily have been obscured by rules and regulations and observing the traditions of the elders—the traditions of washing cups and pots and vessels of bronze. My people, rend your hearts, rend your hearts and not your garments. We've been rending our garments too much of late; we've been making too much of the external trappings and of outer changes; it's high time we got to the heart of the matter.

So now, for me at any rate, Christianity is quite as single–

minded as Zen. It's just a question of conversion, individual and communal; and the rest follows after that. I suppose the Council was getting at this when it said that exterior changes would be useless without a change of heart. Zen reminds us of all this, and it can do a great service to Christians. And I also believe that we Christians can be of service to Zen, especially to those people who are willing to listen to the voice of the great guru who gave us the Sermon on the Mount. At the great turning-points in history (and who will deny that we are at one today?) the world has always looked for men and women with vision and enlightenment. Perhaps by mutual cooperation Buddhism and Christianity can produce such people, whose lives will be relevant and meaningful for our time.

APPENDIX: POSTURE
(Figures appear on pages 106 and 107.)

It is not good to make a fetish of bodily posture, as though it were the whole of meditation. It sometimes happens, even to people far advanced, that a physical handicap prevents the taking-up of one of the recognized postures. Such people can still meditate in the Zen way. Indeed Zen and contemplation can be, and frequently are, practiced on a sick bed. But granted this, the fact remains that the traditional postures are of great value for those who can make use of them.

Figures 1 and 2 show the lotus posture.* This position is very old; it antedates Buddhism in India and has been discovered through archaeological research in ancient Egypt. One places the left foot on the right thigh and the right foot on the left thigh, sways slightly from side to side and then sits in an upright yet relaxed position. The head may be very slightly tilted forward and the eyes can be fixed on a point or not focused at all. Some Christians like to fix their eyes on a crucifix placed on the ground a few feet in front of them. This does not mean that they are thinking and reflecting about the meaning of the crucifix—the crucifix is simply there. This posture has great symbolical meaning. As the lotus rises out of the slime and dirt of the pond, so the bodhisattva rises out of the illusion of the world into the serene beauty of truth. For Christians this posture may also sym-

* The author wishes to express his gratitude to Miss Miwako Kimura who kindly drew the sketches.

Figure 1

Figure 2

Figure 3

Figure 4

Figure 5

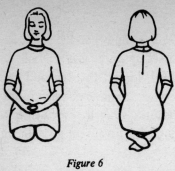

Figure 6

Figure 7

Figure 8

Figure 9

bolize the life of Christ within: "I live, now not I but Christ liveth in me." Self dies and Christ rises up as the center of all.

In Figures 1 and 2, the left hand is held over the right and the thumbs are lightly touching. However in Figure 3 the hands are held open beside the knees. This posture is not used in Zen but is popular in India. Some Christians like it because it gives them a sense of openness before God.

For those who cannot practice the full lotus there is the half-lotus (Figure 4). This is quite as good as the full–lotus and is used by some Zen Masters. In this position it is useful to sit on a somewhat higher cushion; otherwise the knees may be slightly raised, and in order that balance be maintained the knees should touch the ground.

Figure 5 shows an easier way of sitting cross-legged. It is not much used in Japan but is widely used in other Asian countries.

Figure 6 shows the traditional Japanese squatting position called *seiza*, and Figures 7 and 8 show some variations of this. The use of the cushion or small stool makes easier a position which otherwise becomes painful. Even the Japanese are beginning to find difficulty with the traditional postures, so various experiments are being made to find bodily positions that will be reasonably possible for modern people while retaining the advantages of the old postures.

Figure 9 shows how Zen can be practiced in a chair. The chair is seldom used in the temple except by Western people who cannot sit in any of the traditional ways. Our Zen–Christian dialogues have often been held in buildings where sitting on the floor is scarcely feasible. On these occasions we have practiced Zen in the position here sketched.

Glancing at the above postures one can see some features common to all of them. *The back* is always kept straight. This is of great importance. When the back is straight, the breathing auto-

matically becomes abdominal and slows down. A young Buddhist in charge of a meditation hall told me that he could judg
from the back whether or not a person was having distracti
If the back begins to sag, this is a sure sign that the perso
lost inner unification. *The eyes* are kept half-closed. If th
completely closed one easily gets distractions or falls asl
eyes need not be focused at all; or they can be fixed
cifix placed on the ground some distance away. The
of *the breathing* has already been stressed. One may
or repeat an aspiration with the breathing. The re
word "Jesus" is a form of prayer that is traditional in
church and is taught in the *Philokalia* as well as in the fame.
little Russian classic *The Way of a Pilgrim*. In the *Philokalia* it
is said that with the breathing Jesus comes in and "I" go out;
and in this way Christ becomes the center of my life. As progress
is made, however, it may not be necessary to count or to use
words at all. It is enough to be conscious of the fact that one is
breathing—this is called "following the breath." Most people
who practice Zen–type meditation need from time to time to fall
back on something concrete (either an ejaculation or consciousness of the breathing or a *koan*) lest they get completely distracted. Words may be used just as much as is necessary to
maintain unified inner silence without distraction.

POSTSCRIPT

A WAY OF MEDITATION

I

Some people have asked me to write a how-to-do-it book about Christian meditation; and it seems that such a book would fulfill a real need in the modern world. Yet I recoil from this task because I know that meditation is different from cookery and can only be taught by that great teacher whom Augustine calls the *Magister Internus*, the Master Within. Listen to his voice and you will learn how to meditate.

Granted this, however, it is also true that human guide lines can be given; and so I propose to set down some principles or directives which may be of use to people in search of meditation. In doing so I will rely not on my own experience and wisdom but on the words of the Master himself who spoke with such authority that the people were astonished. And I will draw inspiration primarily from the Sermon on the Mount which appeals not only to Christians and Jews but also to many Zen Buddhists and fervent Hindus. By taking to heart and putting into practice the terse advice of Jesus in the fifth, sixth and seventh chapters of *Saint Matthew*, we can be introduced to the royal road of meditation and led to the most profound enlightenment.

Consider the words of Jesus: " Therefore I tell you, do not be anxious about your life, what you shall eat or what you shall drink, nor about your body, what you shall put on" (Mt. 6:25).

When you sit down to meditate, the first thing is to let go
of your anxieties. And when I say anxieties, I include reasoning and thinking and preoccupation and planning and all the
rest. Just let them go. Nor is this easy. For, as we all know, the
human mind is restless. It looks to the future with fear or an-
ticipation; it looks to the past with nostalgia or with guilt.
Seldom does it remain in the here and now. Yet Jesus tells us
clearly to drop anxiety about the future in order to remain in
the present. "Therefore do not be anxious about tomorrow, for
tomorrow will be anxious for itself. Let the day's own trouble
be sufficient for the day" (Mt. 6:34).

And so the first thing is to let go of all preoccupation. Of
course anxieties may flood into your mind. If so, listen to the
practical advice of a great Zen Master: " If you want to obtain
perfect calmness in your zazen, you should not be bothered by
the various images you find in your mind. Let them come, and
let them go. Then they will be under control. But this policy
is not so easy. It sounds easy, but it requires some special effort.
How to make this effort is the secret of practice. . . ."* And
again: "When you are practising zazen, do not try to stop
your thinking. Let it stop by itself. If something comes into
your mind, let it come in and let it go out. It will not stay long.
When you try to stop thinking, it means you are bothered by
it. Do not be bothered by anything."† Yes, do not be bothered
by anything!

If you wish you can simply repeat to yourself the words of
the Lord: "Do not be anxious", "Do not be anxious" . . . Or,
again, some people like to use the words of Peter at the Transfiguration, "Lord, it is good for us to be here" (Mt. 17:4). Any

* *Zen Mind, Beginner's Mind*, Shunryu Suzuki (Tokyo: Weatherhill 1970),
p. 28.
† Ibid., p. 30.

words of sacred scripture, repeated again and again with relish, can be an excellent form of meditation; and they will succeed in warding off all anxiety and needless thinking and reasoning. Moreover, this simple process brings us into the present moment.

As I have said, you will ordinarily be aware of your thoughts and anxieties and you will know that they are in your mind. But do not cling to them. The process is not unlike that taught by Carl Rogers when he tells us (and he is speaking in the context of interpersonal relations) to be *aware* of our anger or frustration or boredom or fear or embarrassment. Be aware of them, he says, and you can handle them. And in the same way, you can be aware of the thoughts in your mind during meditation without clinging to them. As Master Suzuki says, let them come and let them go. Look at them as if they belonged to someone else. This sounds simple; but how difficult it is! For we love our anxieties; we cling to them and wallow in them. We need the advice of Jesus: "Do not be anxious . . ." His words will gradually teach us the gentle art of letting go.

II

Letting go of anxieties, however, is the negative aspect of meditation. In the same context Jesus continues with a very positive assertion: "Is not life more than food, and the body more than clothing?" (Mt. 6:25).

These words abound in common sense. Look out the window and you see a world which is crazy about food and clothing and gas and economic progress. Yet all these things, however desirable and even necessary, are peripheral. What matters is life. What matters is the body. Without a body pulsating with life, of what use are the oil and the tin and the copper and the rubber and the other things? And in meditation we come to

experience our life and our body. We come home to ourselves
and get in touch with what is deepest within us. But first let me
speak of *life*.

In all the great cultures life is symbolized by breath. It is
precisely in experiencing your breath that you experience your
life. So just sit quietly with your back straight and *become
aware of your breathing*. At first do not interfere with it. Do
not attempt to make it short or long or to hold it. In the
pranayama of yoga such breathing exercises exist; but I do not
recommend them here. Only be aware of your breathing as it
is; and, if you wish, you can repeat to yourself : "Breathe in :
breathe out". That is all. Or you can repeat to yourself the
words of the Lord : "Is not life more than food?" The emphasis,
of course, is on *life*.

In this context let me quote a classical Buddhist text which
is very instructive for Christians or for anyone who wants to
learn a simple form of breathing meditation :

A monk who has gone to a forest or the root of a tree or to
an empty place, sits down cross-legged, holding his back
erect, and arouses mindfulness in front of him. Mindful he
breathes in, mindful he breathes out. Whether he is breathing in a long or a short breath, he comprehends that he is
breathing in a long or a short breath. Similarly when he is
breathing out. He trains himself thinking : "I shall breathe
in. I shall breathe out, clearly perceiving the whole body; I
shall breathe in, breathe out, tranquillizing the activity of the
body" . . . For in breathing in or out a long or a short breath
the monk comprehends that he is doing so . . . and he lives
independently of and not grasping anything in the world.*

* See *Buddhist Texts Through the Ages*, Edward Conze, ed. (Oxford, 1954),
pp. 56, 57.

Here, as is evident, one is simply aware ("mindful" is the great Buddhist word) of the natural process of breathing: "I will breathe in: I will breathe out". And this can be done at any time. Sitting in the bus, waiting in a queue, listening to a boring lecture, you can meditate by just breathing in and breathing out. How simple! Yet this practice will give you inner peace, inner strength, inner dignity. It will put you in touch with your deepest self. You may begin to experience in your body the words of Jesus: "Is not life more than food . . .?"

As time goes on, the breathing of its own accord becomes deep and abdominal. Here let me observe that the abdomen (or *hara* as it is called in Japanese) is the vital center of the body in all forms of oriental meditation. If certain western writers have made a huge joke of the so-called navel-gazing of oriental mystics—as though the thing were completely absurd—this does not make it foolish. Oriental mystics do not contemplate their navel in the subject-object sense; but the Sino-Japanese tradition has always taught that life and energy well up from the *tanden*, the point which lies about an inch below the navel —which is expressively called the *kikai* or "ocean of energy". And *tanden breathing* is basic not only to meditation but also to judo, fencing, archery, flower-arrangement, tea-ceremony, calligraphy and the rest.

Let me quote the advice of a Zen Master on this point: "Sit quite still, breathe gently, giving out long breaths, the strength in the lower belly."* And again: "Many of our people breathe through their mouths. But everyone should breathe through the nose and press the breath down into the *tanden*."† Breath, then, is of cardinal importance in Zen. One begins with *tanden*

* See *Hara*, K. Graf Von Durckheim (London: George Allen & Unwin, 1962), p. 178.
† Ibid, p. 179.

breathing but eventually this breathing seems to extend to the whole body. That is why some masters speak of "breathing through every pore"; and a Chinese proverb states that the wise man breathes from his heels. And another interesting point : observation of the breath enters into spiritual direction. A good master carefully watches the breathing (sometimes his eyes are piercing and hawk-like) and from this he judges the spiritual progress and degree of enlightenment of his disciple.*

One does not attain to awareness of breathing overnight. It takes time. But if one perseveres one gradually comes to realize that this breath is not only the life that fills the body from head to toe. It is more. The sanksrit *prana*, like the Japanese *ki*, is *the breath of the universe*, a cosmic force which penetrates all things. As for the Hebrews, they believed that their breath was the breath of God whose presence gave them life. For Christians the breath, like the wind, symbolizes the Holy Spirit who fills all things with his love, giving wisdom and joy and peace.

And so, while breathing, you can recite the words : "Come, Holy Spirit", "Come, Holy Spirit", asking to be filled with the breath of the Spirit. And when this happens, you are not only present to yourself, you are also present to God and to a world which is filled with God and in which God is the deepest reality. You may remain quietly in God's presence reciting these words

---

* It is interesting to recall here that scientists distinguish between the voluntary and involuntary nervous system. There are bodily functions which are voluntary in that we only perform them by an act of the will; and there are others (such as digestion, heart-beat, metabolism and so on) which are involuntary or automatic. And breathing stands mid-way between the two. With most people it is involuntary but it can easily be made conscious, regulated and brought under control of the will. When one becomes conscious of the breathing one gradually becomes conscious of the whole body and even learns to control the whole body. Breathing is the gateway to the unconscious.

—or without words at all. Your breathing may slow down. Or it may even seem to stop. Or a time may come when the indwelling Spirit prompts you to exclaim: "Jesus is Lord!" Such prayers, welling up from the depths of one's being at the prompting of the Spirit, are frequently mentioned in the New Testament. "Abba, Father!" is yet another.

Furthermore, one who is filled with the Spirit may, and must, communicate this same Spirit to others. Remember how Jesus *breathed on his apostles* with the words: "Receive the Holy Spirit" (Jn. 20:22). Cannot we simply sit and breathe good will and healing power to all men, sending them the Spirit? Or we can breathe out love to our friends, imagining that they are present and that we are laying hands on them. Some people like to imagine that they are breathing through their hands, as they communicate the Holy Spirit through this most symbolical action.

Yet another phrase which can be repeated again and again is the Pauline: "For me to live is Christ" (Phil. 1:21). For Paul life was Christ. And we can say the same thing. Yet the profound mystery of these words will not reveal itself to the mere scholar but only to one who is enlightened by the wisdom of the indwelling Spirit. "Come, Holy Spirit."

III

Jesus speaks not only about life but also about the body: "Is not the body more than clothing?" (Mt. 6:25).

Yes. The body is the thing. Any scientist will tell you that the human body is a baffling mystery which no man can fathom. Any theologian will tell you that the body of Christ (a theme that is dear to the heart of Paul) is a mystery of mysteries. And while Sino-Japanese thought will never solve these mysteries, it may teach us a new approach to them; it may teach us to experience and appreciate this precious gift which we call the human body; it may teach us to be present to ourselves and to reality and to God through the body.

Body-awareness can be achieved, as I have already indicated, by breathing from one's heels. But it can also be achieved through posture. And this is one of the great arts of the eastern world, having its roots in *hatha yoga* with its rich variety of *asanas* or bodily postures through which one is brought to enlightenment. Chief among these is the lotus, which is called "the perfect posture" and has been widely used throughout Asia from pre-historic times. Perfect indeed it is because, correctly practiced, it unites mind and body like two sides of one coin and brings one into a state of total liberation.

To sit in the lotus is an art and an accomplishment which takes time and patience and spiritual training. But once we learn the art of sitting, we discover that the very posture is enlightenment. Here we have a species of *enlightenment through the body*. Listen again to Shunryu Suzuki speaking about the lotus: "To take this posture itself is the purpose of our practice. When you have this posture, you have the right state of mind, so there is no need to try to attain some special state"* And again: "The state of mind that exists when you sit in the right posture is, itself, enlightenment."† It is indeed an enlightenment to sit in the lotus and to realize that the body is more than the clothing.

But at this juncture let me digress for a moment to make an observation that is of cardinal importance for what I am trying to say. We are sometimes told that oriental "techniques" are a marvelous aid to concentration. After all, the nervous and

* Suzuki, p. 22.
† Ibid., p. 24.

jittery occidental needs to relax, to calm down, to take it easy. And once this is done, he can get on with the real job of pray- ing. In other words, oriental breathing and posture are regarded as warming-up exercises, preparations for the real thing.

Now this is an abysmal misunderstanding. What we can learn from the East is not just preparatory devices but the art of prayer itself. For the Orient can teach us to pray with our breathing, to pray with our body, to pray with our whole being. After all, God created the whole person, not just the mind; and he should be adored by the whole person, not just by the mind. In the past few centuries, prayer in the West became inexcusably cerebral (though it was not so in the middle-eastern Church where Hesychasm was born) but now at last we are re-learning the art of adoring God with mind and body and breathing. We are allowing faith to fill not only our mind but also our breath and our *hara* and our body. And it is here that the East can help us.

As I have already indicated, in Sino-Japanese thought, the center of gravity of the body is the *tanden*, the point about an inch below the navel which is the elixir of life and the sea of energy. One should breathe from the *tanden*—not in the sense that the breath actually penetrates to that region of the body, but that one imagines that it does. And gradually one gets a sense of the *tanden* together with a balance and harmony and quietude that fill the whole person. An old Zen Master, stating that the *tanden* is the shrine of the divine, asserts that the woes of humanity are caused by lack of balance. He then goes on to divide mankind into three classes.

To the first class belong those who value their heads. Such people develop bigger and bigger heads until they topple over like a pyramid standing upside down. Such people obviously have little power or creativity. How could they possibly maintain balance?

In the second class are those who value their chest. This is the military type that seems to be ascetic and disciplined but is, in fact, easily overcome.

To the third class belong those who value the belly or *hara* and build their strength there. These are the people with calmness, peace and strength. They are (and this is an old eastern ideal) people who follow their natural inclinations without breaking the law. To sit with the strength in the *hara* is authentic Zen.

The men and women who practice the martial arts such as judo, archery, fencing and the like, learn to hold their attention at the *tanden* and to stand with firmness and power.* They, like the practitioners of Zen, wear the traditional *hakama* the sash of which is knotted just at the *tanden*. And there are various forms of "*tanden* practice". Of these an interesting one is the simple art of polishing a table—doing so with large circular sweeps and holding the attention at the *tanden*, not at the polishing hand, until one gradually gets a sense of the whole body and feels fully alive.

And so one learns body-awareness and posture: how to sit, how to stand, how to walk, how to breathe, how to relax. One acts with the whole body. Needless to say, this is not just a prerogative of the Orient. I know of western pianists and painters and writers who act from the hips and from their whole body, not just from the head. But whereas the West has stumbled on this sense of the body, the East has cultivated it assiduously for centuries.

* Note that I say "men and women". All that I say about posture and breathing applies equally to men and women.

And yet paradoxically the climax of *tanden* practice is reached when, forgetting one's body and one's self, one allows the universe to act. In traditional archery there is a saying that the action of releasing the arrow should be an action not of the individual but of the universe. And in the same way one who practices Zen for a long time comes to the stage where he does not bother about the *tanden* or the breathing or the body or the self. He comes to experience not that "I am breathing" but that "The universe is breathing". The self has gone.

Yet another result of this training is that one comes to experience a great *wisdom of the body*. One whose mind is attuned to his body finds that the body tells him when to eat and when to fast, when to sleep and when to watch, when to work and when to meditate. The body is a mysterious and marvellous instrument; it has powers and potentialities which western science has not dreamed of (though now it begins to suspect their existence)—powers which no computer can possess. But we must train this body, be attuned to it, listen to its wisdom. "Is not . . . the body more than clothing?"

Practically speaking, one way of meditating is to adopt one of the postures which I have described in this book as a way to bodily awareness. Become aware of your hands and your feet and your whole body, quietly repeating the words of Jesus: "Is not . . . the body more than clothing?" Do not think and reason about these words. Just relish or savor them while being aware that this body is more than the clothing. The fact that the words you use are from the Gospels puts you in contact with Christ and makes your prayer one of faith. Furthermore the word "body" may speak more and more powerfully if you

are aware (but again in a non-discursive way) of the mystery of
the body of Christ. This is the body which has become one with
my body. "He who eats my flesh and drinks my blood abides
in me, and I in him" (Jn. 6:56). This is the body which
is "the fullness of him who fills all in all" (Ephes. 2:23). Just
as the breath of Jesus is the breath of the universe, so the
body of Jesus is one with the universe. "Is not the body
more than clothing?" There may come a time when body
and breathing and ego are forgotten and our true self cries
out with St. Paul: "I live, now not I but Christ lives in me"
(Gal. 2:20).

IV

I said that the first step in meditation consists in letting go
of anxieties and fears and grasping of all kind. And I quoted
the words of Jesus: "Do not be anxious . . ."

Now I can hear someone say: "Well and good! This sounds
fine. But is it possible? Can I let go of fears and anxieties? After
all, any psychologist will tell you that anxiety is deeply rooted
in the human psyche. It is engrained in the memory, going right
back to the primal scream which we uttered when we emerged
from the womb. As we pass through layers of consciousness
in meditation, new anxieties—or old repressed anxieties—will
rise to the surface of the mind. And you tell me just to sit and
let go! Is it quite so simple?"

This is a very valid objection. And in answer to it I would
again quote the Sermon on the Mount which emphasizes one
enormously important point: *faith*. "O men of little faith"
(Mt. 6:25). Jesus speaks here of the faith which tells you that
your Father is looking after you, that he is protecting you—
faith that you are loved. Yes, you may be the biggest sinner in

the world. You may have committed the most heinous crimes; but you are loved by your Father who "makes his sun rise on the evil and on the good, and sends rain on the just and on the unjust" (Mt. 5:45). And I can let go of anxieties as the conviction of being loved grows and deepens and becomes an unshakable source of strength.

Jesus put it very poetically. " But if God so clothes the grass of the field, which today is alive and tomorrow is thrown into the oven, will he not much more clothe you, O men of little faith?" (Mt. 6:30). Your Father who protects the birds of the air will much more protect you because you are of greater value than they. You are of immense value.

I am loved. I am of great value. To accept this is the great act of faith. For it is well known that many, too many, people despise themselves, find that they are overcome with gnawing guilt and a morbid sense of unworthiness. And to them Jesus says: "Do not be anxious. You are important. You are of value. If the flowers and the birds are valuable (and they are), how much more value are you!"

Now all this is the greatest practical importance. When you sit to meditate, recall your personal dignity—Remember that you are of the greatest value. "I'm O.K.: you're O.K." To foster this attitude of mind it will help to meditate in surroundings which will create an atmosphere of inner security. It will help to choose a quiet place; to wear suitable clothing. Above all, it will help to adopt a posture that expresses your dignity and gives you a sense of being O.K. And then you can quietly repeat the words of Jesus which I have just quoted. Or you can recite the words from Jeremiah: "I have loved you with an everlasting love" (Jer. 31:3). Or the words of Jesus: "Let not your hearts be troubled; believe in God, believe also in me" (Jn. 14:1). Sacred Scripture abounds in phrases which tell us to have faith and not to be afraid. " Do not be afraid. It is I" (Jn. 6 : 20) "God is love" (Jn. 4 : 16).

And through the savoring and relishing of these words, faith enters into one's mind and heart and body and breath, becoming co-extensive with one's being. Sometimes there may be moments of great joy and liberation when, freed from anxiety, one can exclaim with Paul : "He loved me and gave himself for me" (Gal. 2 : 20).

Let me repeat that I am not saying that one should reason and think about faith. Only that one should sit silently, receiving the love of God into the depths of one's being. "And in praying do not heap up empty phrases as the Gentiles do; for they think that they will be heard for their many words. Do not be like them. . . ." (Mt. 6 : 7). Faith does not need a lot of words. Just as a man who knows that he is loved by a woman, or a woman who knows that she is loved by a man, carries this conviction constantly without reasoning about it, so one who believes he is loved by God does not need to think a lot. The principal thing is to receive and to keep receiving the immense love which is being offered, which *threatens* to inundate us and from which we fly as we fly from the hound of heaven.

Perhaps we could say that the basis of Christian meditation is the art of being loved. If someone has written a book called *The art of loving*, perhaps someone else could write one on *The art of being loved*. It would teach people to open their hearts to love, both human and divine; not to put obstacles in the way. *The Song of Songs* speaks of opening the door to the Beloved. And Jesus says: "Behold, I stand at the door and knock; if any one hears my voice and opens the door . . ." (Rev. 3 : 20). If we are to meditate we must learn the art of sitting silently with the door open.

And let us remember that the love of God, received in meditation, makes us more and more O.K. For it purifies; it redeems; it justifies (if I may use the Pauline term) and makes us holy. Mystics like the author of *The Cloud* tells us that contemplation makes us beautiful not only in the sight of God but also in the sight of men and women who have eyes to recognize this kind of beauty. And Paul calls the brethren "saints".

I have spoken about Christian faith. But what about the role of faith in Buddhist meditation? What about the role of faith in Zen?

No doubt some of my readers will think there is no faith in Zen and little faith in any form of Buddhism. Popular literature on the subject has given this impression. It prefers to emphasize human potential rather than faith—because this is what the West is looking for. Besides, human potential sells better than faith.

But in fact Buddhism is based on faith. This is particularly true of Pure Land Buddhism which arose in North India at the beginning of the Christian era and became extremely popular throughout Asia—the Pure Land is a religion of faith, of pure faith. The Buddha Amida, it holds, has made a vow to save all sentient beings who call upon his name with faith. In other words, one who recites the name (and this recitation of the name is called the *nembutsu*) with faith in Amida will be liberated from bad *karma* and reborn in the Pure Land. And so among Buddhists of this persuasion there exists a form of meditation which consists simply in reciting the name again and again and again with devotion and trust and faith in the mercy of Amida and in the efficacy of his vow. The resemblance to the Christian "Jesus prayer" is so obvious that I need not dwell on it here.

As for Zen, the masters constantly exhort to *great faith*. This faith is summed up in an incantation which is constantly recited in the temple and runs as follows :

> I put my faith in the Buddha
> I put my faith in the *dharma*
> I put my faith in the *sangha*

Since the *dharma* means the law; and the *sangha* means the community, this triple invocation could be paralleled in the Christian life by the prayer :

> I put my faith in Jesus
> I put my faith in the Bible
> I put my faith in the Church

I believe that without these three elements of basic faith authentic religious meditation is not possible.

My reader will observe the great stress on the holy books : the *sutras* and the Bible. Christians and Buddhists who seriously meditate must constantly recite their holy books with love and devotion. Again there is the stress on community. This community may be a small group indeed (it may even consist of husband and wife) but it is part of the larger group which is the Church. Without it, meditation easily wanders off into the mists of illusion.

Of course the Buddhist way of speaking about faith is often baffling to the uninitiated. Shunryu Suzuki, for example, can write : "I discovered that it is necessary, absolutely necessary to believe in nothing. That is, we have to believe in something which has no form and no color—something which exists before all forms and colors appear."*

In saying that it is necessary to believe in nothing, Suzuki means (and this is clear from his ensuing pages) that it is

* Suzuki, p. 112.

necessary to *cling* to nothing—not to say any ideas of God or thoughts of God. But yet it is necessary to believe in something without form. Suzuki is here proposing something that is very close to the pure or naked faith of St. John of the Cross. But I cannot enter into that here because discussion of Buddhist nothingness would take us too far afield.

Now obviously Buddhist faith and Christian faith are different, as the Buddha differs from Jesus and the *dharma* from the gospel. Nevertheless they have something in common. What is the common denominator?

I myself believe that it is the inner conviction that everything is well. Clearly no authentic Buddhist will say that all is well because *God loves the world*; but he will claim an inner security based on the conviction that everything is alright— an inner security which stands in the midst of suffering, earthquake, flood, famine and war. It looks all wrong but in fact all is well. "All will be well and all will be well and all manner of thing will be well" wrote Juliana of Norwich; and her refrain was taken up by T. S. Eliot in *Four Quartets*. It is a refrain that pulsates through the meditation of Christian and Buddhist alike.

And so I suggest that the Christian who wishes to meditate sit constantly with the conviction that all is well, that he is loved by God. Let him advance in the pure and naked and silent faith that liberates from anxiety.

V

I am trying to say that when we read the Sermon on the Mount we should do what Jesus tells us to do rather than thinking about the meaning of his words. Just follow his advice! You remember that he says: "Look at the birds of the air ..." (Mt. 6:26), and: "Consider the lilies of the field ... (Mt. 6:28). Well, take this literally. Look at the grass; look at the flowers; look at the birds. Just take a good look. Many people have never really looked at anything. While looking at things they are thinking about something else. The result is that they don't really see the beauty that lies around them—the beauty in nature and the beauty in persons.

Now Zen speaks about "just looking", "just listening", "just sitting". This means that you look or listen or sit and do nothing else. Perhaps we could call it "pure looking". Or Zen will tell us just to listen—to the sound of the river or the waterfall or the rain or whatever it may be. Just listen and do nothing else but listen. And in doing this you become one with the object: you identify with it: you lose your small self and discover your true self.

I have sometimes practiced this kind of meditation with students. Smoggy Tokyo is not the best place in the world to look at birds or to relish the beauty of the flowers. But nevertheless Sophia University has a small garden. We go there in silence and each one simply picks up a stone or a flower or some object of nature—and looks at it, touches it, smells it, becomes it. "Look at the birds of the air ..." (Mt. 6:26). The Greek word *emblepo* which is used in the text does not mean to look in a casual or absent-minded way: it means to have a good look, to penetrate into, to see into the heart of the thing. It reminds me of the way in which a Zen master tells his disciple to look at a *koan*, to look at it with mind and body, to grapple with it, to become one with it. It is in this way that the inner eye is opened and one comes to self-realization.

It is said that the Bodhisattva Kannon got enlightenment by

just listening to every sound. The name *kannon*, originally *Kanze-on*, means literally "the one who listens to the sounds of the world". And so Kannon was just listening, totally present to reality and its sounds. What a tremendous *awareness* or *mindfulness* was here! But there is another translation of the name which is even more remarkable. Instead of "the one who listens to the *sounds* of the world", there is a translation which runs "the one who listens to the *cries* of the world". In other words, Kannon listens to the cries of the poor and the sick and the dying. He takes these cries into the depth of his being and identifies with them. This is compassion; and this is enlightenment. If we could imitate Kannon in listening to the cries of the poor in our day how close we would be to the Kingdom of God!

But let me return to the Sermon on the Mount. Jesus tells us to consider the lilies of the field and then to reflect on our own value and dignity. "Are you not of more value than they?" (Mt. 6:26). Now we could take these words in a discursive way, comparing ourselves with the lilies and the birds. We could say that in the scale of evolution we are one step higher and, in consequence, are much more valuable. And then we could reflect on God's great love and care for us, thus becoming conscious of our dignity as men and women. This is the discursive approach to the text.

But can we not approach the same text in a contemplative way? When we do so, we realize that in contemplating the lily we become the lily and realize our true value: in looking at the bird we become the bird and realize our true worth. Again let me return to Zen. In listening to the waterfall I may get a ray of enlightenment: not about the beauty of the waterfall as such but about myself as listening and not separate. Listening, like looking, is thus a way to self-realization. And Jesus, too, is saying that in looking at the lily, in becoming the lily, I realize my true self—I realize that I am loved by my Father and that I am of great value.

VI

All that I have said so far is leading in one direction : namely, towards contemplative prayer. It is upon this that all Christian ways converge. Yet here permit me to recall something I said at the beginning of this Postscript, when I insisted that the principal teacher of prayer is the *Magister Internus* or Master Within. Now this is particularly true of contemplative prayer. It is not taught by man alone. It is a call, a vocation, an invitation to ascend to a privileged seat in the banquet of love.

The earlier stages of contemplative prayer are characterized by the sense of presence—the sense that God is near, that he loves, that "in Him we live and move and have our being" (Acts 17:28). The author of *The Cloud* speaks of a blind stirring of love that arises in the heart and draws one into the cloud of unknowing beyond all thought and image and ratiocination. One is held by this blind stirring of love (St. John of the Cross calls it the living flame of love) in a way that is similar to the silence of lovers who need no words because they are united in intuitive intimacy. And this stirring of love gives birth to a wisdom that guides us, enlightens us, tells us what to do and what not to do in daily life. Under the guidance of love one knows intuitively what to do in concrete circumstances.

When this blind stirring of love arises in the heart, one must follow it with great freedom. One may find oneself forgetting about breathing and awareness exercises just as one forgets about the reasoning and thinking of the discursive intellect. All this kind of thing is buried beneath a cloud of forgetting. Now

one follows the inner light with complete liberty. Of this stage
St. John of the Cross writes :

> Here there is no longer any way.
> For the just man there is no way.
> He is a law unto himself.

Here there is no way! It is always a snare to cling to ways and
methods. When the time comes, when we hear the voice of the
Master who knocks at the door, then we must leave all methodology to open the door to one who comes in and dines with us
and we with him.

This inner stirring of love may well up in acts of praise or
thanksgiving or petition or trust or love or whatever. But at
other times it may be totally silent and wordless. It may consist
in loving converse—what the old authors call "intimacy with
God"; or it may be that, silent and without words, I am "naked
of self and clothed with Christ" offering myself to the Father
for the salvation of the human race.

Now while this experience of loving contemplation or loving
knowledge has much in common with Zen, I do not believe it
is the same. In other words I do not think that Christian contemplation and Zen are "the same thing"; and I believe that
most Zen Masters (and perhaps all authentic Zen Masters) will
agree with me here. For one thing Zen never speaks of love.
Some Christian writers, it is true, will say that although there
is no talk of love in Zen, still Zen is love-filled and simply uses
another terminology. And at one time I myself thought in this
way. But when I proposed this theory I never found an authentic Zen person willing to go along with it. For them, sentiments
of love for God, even for a God who is my deepest being and
my truest self, are a species of illusion or *makyo*. I believe that

this comes out in the interview with the Roshi about which I wrote in the first chapter of this book.

Now while it is true that when the Christian contemplative life develops, the sense of presence may become a sense of absence, the light may become darkness and the sentiments of love may wither and dry up—still, this is only towards the summit when one cries out: "My God, my God, why has thou forsaken me?" (Mt. 27:46). Here one is in emptiness and darkness and nothingness and the void. Here all the words of oriental mysticism apply. But still there remains a belief, a profound belief, in a God who, though seemingly absent, *should* be present. Here the blind stirring of love has become very blind indeed and very dark. But love is still there. And the 22nd psalm from which these words are taken ends with a cry of joy and praise and thanksgiving:

> I will tell of thy name to my breathen;
> in the midst of the congregation I will praise thee
>
> (Psalm 22:22)

These are the words of one who has passed through the desert and has once again a deep experience of the nearness and presence of God.

For me, then, the greatest practical difference between Zen and Christian contemplation is that whereas Zen rewards thoughts and feelings and aspirations of love for God as so much *makyo* and illusion, I regard these sentiments as—yes, imperfect and inadequate to express the reality, but nevertheless as true and valid and valuable religious experiences.

And here we are at the crux of the matter: it is one thing to say that sentiments and thoughts of God are inadequate: it is another thing to say that they are illusory. It is one thing to say that thoughts and sentiments must be transcended: it is another thing to say they must be rejected. And it was because of this delicate but important distinction that I myself found it impossible to practice "pure Zen" or "Buddhist Zen" with authenticity. From Zen I can, and will continue to, learn many things. But I am convinced that it is not the same as the Christian contemplation to which I feel called.*

At one point where the author of *The Cloud* is making a subtle distinction he cautiously observes: "Be careful of errors here, I beg you. Remember that the nearer a man comes to the truth, the more sensitive he must become to error."† I apply this to Zen and Christian contemplation. Precisely because the differences are so fine and subtle we must all the more beware of error.

VII

In the Sermon on the Mount, Jesus issues a solemn warning: "Beware of practicing your piety before men in order to be seen by them . . ." (Mt. 6:1). He is speaking, of course, about the hypocrites who stand in the synagogue or at the street corner looking for praise and attention. "Truly, I say to you, they have their reward" (Mt. 6:5).

To look for recognition and praise, to search for success, to glory in achievement—these are very natural human tendencies. But they are the great snare in the things of the spirit. And here is the temptation which besets the meditation move-

* St. John of the Cross insists that thoughts of God are not God; sentiments and feelings of God are not God; images of God are not God. All these are imperfect and must be transcended. But to say they are imperfect is not to say they are false or illusory.

† *The Cloud of Unknowing*, William Johnston, ed. (New York: Doubleday, 1973).

ment which has spread throughout the world today. So much of this meditation movement is geared to achievement of all kinds—to the development of human potential, to success in interpersonal relations, to attainment of enlightenment or illumination—that the great temptation is to cry out in the church or at the street corner: "I got enlightenment; I made the grade. Here is my diploma." And to this Jesus answers: "Truly, I say to you, you have your reward." After all you are now recognized by men—do you also want recognition from God?

Purity of intention, on the other hand, is a virtue which is stressed throughout Asian spirituality from the time of the *Bhagavad Gita*. One of the main points of the *Gita* (and a point which was dear to the heart of Gandhi) is that we should work without seeking the fruit of our labor. In other words, we devote ourselves to right action without caring about success or failure; and this non-attachment gives us a joy and a liberty which is an unlooked-for reward. And what the *Gita* says of action is equally or more true of meditation. You are not trying *to get something*; you are not looking for results. Much less are you looking for recognition. You are engaging in perfect action which is its own reward. In short, the perfection of action in total liberty is the great ideal.

And the same ideal is present in the traditional Sino-Japanese martial arts like archery and fencing and judo. We moderns naturally think that the aim is to hit the bull's eye or to defeat one's opponent. Not so. The aim is perfect action, total liberation, loss of self. The arrow will go straight to its mark; but that is not one's aim. It is just like authentic Zen where one must never look for results. There are early monastic exhortations which tell monks deliberately to do good deeds which will never be seen or recognized by anyone. It all reminds one of the "do not let your left hand know what your right hand is doing" (Mt. 6:3).

As I have already indicated, Christian teachers also stress purity of intention as something of the utmost importance. This is because Christian meditation is ultimately an expression of love and in its highest form Christian meditation is pure love, disinterested love. If I love because of some gain or profit, then my love is still imperfect. In one of his minor treatises, the author of *The Cloud* speaks about the woman who is not chaste because she loves her husband for his goods and not for himself. And in the same way if we love God because of the ensuing human potential or inner consolation our love is not chaste.

Perfect love, like perfect action, is its own reward and is for its own sake. That is why Bernard of Clairvaux, that great lover, can cry: "I love because I love; I love in order to love..." How different this is from the cry: "I love because I realize that loving is good for me"! Indeed, there is no reason for love. Love searches for nothing. That is why purity of intention is central to Christian prayer which is an enactment of the commandment to love God with one's whole heart and soul, and to love one's neighbor as one's self.